THE SIX FACES OF LOVE

BY

CRAIG OWEN

ISBN 1-58500-400-6

1stbooks - rev.01/20/00

About the Book

How do you know when you are in love? Why do people confuse romantic and spiritual love? THE SIX FACES OF LOVE answers these and other questions about love and relationships. It discusses the six different forms of love: friendship, romantic, spiritual, community, marital and family love. THE SIX FACES OF LOVE explains what all six loves have in common and what makes each love unique. Many examples of real people with real struggles are used to illustrate the similarities and differences between the six loves.

Spiritual love is the most important of the six loves. Once you understand the nature of spiritual love, you can experience all of the other loves in more fulfilling way. If you have been searching for a love that is fulfilling and lasting, THE SIX FACES OF LOVE will help you find it.

Dedication

To Grandma K. and the things we hoped for and
To Grandma A. who showed me the
meaning of faith.

Acknowledgements

As it takes a village to raise a child, it takes a community of friends to help make an author's idea for a book into a reality. I want to thank Kelly, Valerie, Deanne, Shelley, David and Cynthia, Bonnie and Gary, Joann and Virgil, Kirk and Angi and Mom & Dad for patiently reading through earlier versions of this book. Their feedback and suggestions greatly improved the book. A special thanks goes to Cathy G. for checking the manuscript for grammar and spelling errors. And also my appreciation to Mo and the writers group for teaching me to edit more effectively.

Many other people have helped me in ways great and small. Thank you for your support and I hope you are as proud of the results as am I.

Craig Owen

Table Of Contents

CHAPTER ONE

HOW DO YOU KNOW YOU ARE IN LOVE?

"The essence of Love is a sense of sanctuary"

Cheryl and Peter had been single for several years. Both had both survived unhealthy relationships in the past, and neither believed they would find a truly intimate relationship. Everything changed when they first met one another. Their first three months together were "heaven on earth" according to Cheryl. It felt like they had known each other for years when they had only known each other for a few weeks. Three months into their relationship problems started developing. The thrill of falling in love had faded, they began to see each other's imperfections and their fights became more frequent. Now they were not sure if they loved each other anymore.

What had gone wrong?

Larry and Beth planned to be married once Larry finished college. Their plans were disrupted when Larry survived a serious auto accident. Larry felt he needed to find meaning and purpose in his life before he could marry Beth. He broke their engagement and spent the next several years traveling. After studying philosophy in India and Japan and finding few answers, he drifted back to his hometown and lived with his parents. Larry wandered from one relationship to another, never finding a woman with whom he felt happy. One day he awoke to find that he was 40 years old and very much alone. What had gone wrong in his search for love and purpose in his life?

Kevin and Claire were professors at a small midwestern college. Both were happily married and had families of their own. They developed a close and warm friendship with each other and were very open about it. Kevin and Claire often had lunch together or took walks around the campus. Both of their spouses were aware of their friendship and had no problems with it, but it seemed the students and staff of the college had other ideas. Rumors began circulating that the two of them were having an affair. None of this was true, but the denials made by Kevin and Claire only added fuel to the rumors. Eventually they ended their friendship rather than put up with the incessant rumors. How could the college community be so wrong in their perceptions of the open friendship between Kevin and Claire?

WHY ALL THE CONFUSION?

All of the couples mentioned in the stories above have one thing in common: they are all confused about love. Peter and Cheryl are confused about falling in love which is different from being in love. Larry is confusing spiritual love with romantic love. Expecting to find both in one relationship, he has been unable to find either. Kevin and Claire are the victims of their college community's lack of understanding about friendships between men and women. How can each couple find their way out of confusion about love? The purpose of this book is to answer their questions and confusions about love. But before their confusion can be cleared up we must understand more clearly what we are talking about. What we are talking about are the six different loves.

There are at least six different kinds of love, each with its own distinctive relationship. The six loves are friendship, romance, spiritual, community, marriage and family love. Much of the confusion in relationships comes from looking for the wrong love in the wrong place. Consider the following examples. We may think we are seeking romance with someone when in fact we may be looking for friendship. Many people expect a successful romance to make them happy, but if this is true, why do so many people still feel unhappy even in love? Many religious people feel that they cannot have any friends outside of their religion. Is this really an accurate understanding of spiritual love and the love of friendship? Some 'pop' forms of therapy tell us that we cannot hope to have a successful marriage until we deal with the problems from our past. Yet, it seems that the only people we can find as possible partners all have their own unresolved problems just like us. Is this a cause for hope or hopelessness in finding a partner? To answer these and other questions we must first understand what love is and then carefully look at each of the six different loves.

In this chapter I will offer one possible answer to the question 'How do you know when you are in love?' This is not a question that only interests philosophers, but a very practical question that each of us faces at one time or another. I will offer a definition of love and some principles that I believe all six loves have in common. The following chapters will discuss the characteristics that make each love distinct from the other loves. By sorting out the different loves in this way we can begin to answer some of the questions facing Cheryl and Peter, Larry and Beth and Kevin and Claire. We will return to each of these couples, as well as look at other people very much like them, in the chapters to follow. But for now, I will start with a definition of love.

LOVE DEFINED

How does one answer the question "How do you know when you are in love?" This problem usually arises with romantic love, but it can occur in the other loves as well. Perhaps we can borrow a technique from philosophy to help get us started. A standard method in philosophy is to first carefully define the terms you are discussing. After defining your terms, you arrive at criteria or principles to verify when you have an example of the subject you so carefully defined. Maybe this method of definition and verification can be of help to us.

Here is my definition of love: Love is a choice to be committed, vulnerable, and responsible to the one for whom you care. There are a lot of heavy words in that definition, 'choice,' 'commitment,' 'vulnerable,' 'responsible.' Let us take a careful look at these terms in the order I have given them.

What do I mean when I say love is a choice? Love is a decision we make, a matter of the will. Love is not to be identified with emotions alone. Feelings are certainly a part of love, and our emotional response to people is one way of finding someone we could choose to love. What exactly do we choose to do in loving someone? One of the things we choose is to make a commitment.

When I use the word commitment I do not mean blind devotion such as "My lover right or wrong." One writer describes commitment as "the capacity to dedicate oneself to another person or cause."[1] We choose (there is that word again) to have a personal stake in the growth and life of the one we love. When we make a commitment to the one we love we say to them "I believe in you. I believe in who you are and in who you can become." By saying "I believe in who you are" we accept the one we love, imperfections as well as strengths. In affirming "I believe in who you can become" we recognize that people grow and change, even in love. We challenge, in the name of love, our loved one to grow beyond their comfortable limits for the sake of love. All of this talk of believing, growing, and commitment is risky business. This brings us to our next word, vulnerability.

Being vulnerable in love means that we willingly accept the pain and struggle of love as well as the joy and happiness of love. When we are committed to someone by believing in them, we cannot escape the disappointments and upsets that come with loving imperfect people. The joy of love cannot be separated from the pain of love. Unless we accept this paradox we will run from love every time it becomes painful or difficult. Choosing to be committed and vulnerable to the one you love is a decision to be responsible, the last word in my definition of love.

Responsibility in love means we are accountable to and for the one we love. Being accountable to the one we love involves activities that many of us have trouble with: trusting one another, being honest with each other, communicating (as opposed to just talking) with each other. To be accountable for the one we love is also difficult. There will be times when we must answer for and even defend the one we love. Since we know our loved one so well, sometimes we our obligated to make use of that knowledge. The occasion maybe as dramatic as a life or death medical situation, or as simple as a conversation with friends who ask how our loved one is doing. Being accountable to and for the one we love flies in the face of the self indulgent individualism of our day. Yet, without responsibility love can endure over time.

So now we have our definition of love. Our task is only half completed, however. We could

4

argue endlessly over definitions and words. To avoid this we must arrive at some criteria or principles that will verify that we have an instance of love as we have defined it. The three principles I suggest come out of the experience of other writers who are well acquainted with the human condition.

FIRST PRINCIPLE: HOW DO I NEED YOU?

My first principle comes from Eric Fromm. It is in the form of a question. How do you love the one you love? "Do you love them because you need them, or do you need them because you love them?"[2] Let us look at both sides of this question.

"Do you love them because you need them?" Most of the things we do arise from mixed motives. The majority of our actions are the result of good and bad reasons blended together. (Only saints can claim to act from pure motives, and I have yet to meet one.) Love is no exception to the reality of mixed motives. When we are in love we bring with us our best and worst qualities. The question "Do you love them because you need them?" is meant to scrutinize how predominant are our worst qualities in a love relationship. We all have some subconscious programming that affects how we choose the ones we love. For people with addictive personalities or seriously low self esteem, unhealthy and subconscious programming can be the predominant factor in how they choose the ones they love. If you love someone more because you need them, then beware. You should carefully examine the dynamics of your relationship and why you are attracted to your loved one. You might have some personal issues to work through before you can achieve the kind of love relationship you seek but cannot seem to find.

"Do you need them because you love them?" A slight rewording of the question describes a very different situation. In a relationship where two people deliberately choose to become interdependent, the need for each other can become overwhelming. The difference here is that the good qualities in each person are more predominant in their choice of a loved one. Good qualities such as trust, honesty, communication, and commitment will outweigh the negative qualities of jealousy, insecurity, and anger. As I mentioned before, love will always have mixed motives and qualities. If you need someone because you love them, then the good qualities should more than compensate for the bad.

SECOND PRINCIPLE: WHO AM I?

My second principle is a line from the movie The Accidental Tourist. "It is not just how much you love someone, it is who you are when you are with them."[3] The movie revolves around the struggles of a man named Macon Leary who is a very predictable person. He likes to have everything planned and organized. Macon writes a series of travel guide books called The Accidental Tourist for reluctant business travelers who want to feel safe in their journeys. Whether you are in London or Paris, Macon's books tell you which hotels have the nicest bathrooms and which restaurants serve American food.

Macon's safe and sheltered life is shattered when his wife Sarah decides to move out and get a divorce. Being a quiet and withdrawn person by nature, Macon reacts by becoming even more quiet and withdrawn. He might have gotten away with it except for meeting a woman named Muriel. Muriel is as spontaneous and disorganized as Macon is subdued and predictable. Muriel takes an immediate liking to Macon and keeps pestering him to go out with her. He finally does and falls in love with her. As their relationship grows, Muriel's love for Macon changes him into a new person. He becomes more spontaneous and playful, and his normally dismal attitude about life becomes more hopeful. Towards the end of the movie Macon makes one last attempt to reconcile with his wife Sarah. They move back into their house and try living together again, but it is no use. Macon has changed too much to go back to his old ways. As he explains to Sarah why he wants to go back to Muriel, he tells her "Its not just how much you love someone, but who you are when you are with them." Muriel has given Macon another chance at life by allowing him to decide all over again what kind of person he wants to be.

"I believe in you. I believe in who you are and in who you can become." This is the support and freedom Macon found in his love for Muriel and the hope and freedom we should find in our love relationships. Who are you when you are with the one you love? Do you feel a sense of freedom? Do you find a giddy courage to try new things, to grow beyond your comfortable limits? Or are you a perpetual prisoner of your old fears and insecurities? Is your relationship more like a comfortable pair of shoes that you keep out of familiarity instead of going to the trouble of getting a new pair? I leave you to answer these questions for yourself.

THIRD PRINCIPLE: SANCTUARY

The third and last principle is from a writer who says "the essence of love is a sense of sanctuary." Sanctuary has two distinct aspects, protection and renewal. We each have our fears, insecurities, hurts, and pains that we share with a few people. If we want to grow and change for the better, we need to share these burdens with the person you love. The sense of sanctuary we find in love gives us the protection we need to share our hurts and fears with our loved one. We sense that our loved one will not make a public display of our weaknesses and fears. The protective sanctuary of love is like a mother bird spreading her wings over her young in the nest. Within the warm confines of their mother's wings the young birds know they do not have anything to fear. This feeling that we are safe and everything is okay is the protection we should find in love.

Besides protection, the sanctuary of love also provides a chance for renewal. Sanctuary is not simply an escape from the unpleasant realities of ourselves, for when we share our burdens with others we are re-energized and restrengthened. We no longer carry our pains and fears alone and find strength to overcome those pains and fears. If we cannot overcome them, then we find in our love the ability to live with our burdens instead of grimly enduring them. It must remain a mystery how the love of two people can be greater that the burdens of one. I only know that it is true from my own experience and that of many others.

Our task is now complete. I have given you a definition of love: Love is a choice to be committed, vulnerable and responsible to the one for whom you care. And I have given you three principles by which to judge your love. "Do you love them because you need them, or do you need them because you love them?" "It is not just how much you love someone, but who you are when you are with them." "The essence of love is a sense of sanctuary." I cannot guarantee that this definition and these principles will always lead to love. I do believe that these ideas will give you a place from which to start as you seek to find love in your life.

Now that we have a definition of love in general, where do we begin to discuss the six loves? By starting with the most basic of the six loves, friendship, to which we now turn in the next chapter.

CHAPTER TWO

FRIENDSHIP

"Before kingdoms can change, people must change."

Kevin taught history and Claire taught art at a small midwestern college. They developed a close friendship, often having lunch together or taking walks around the college grounds. Kevin and Claire were open about their relationship, saying they were just friends and that neither of their spouses had problems with their friendship. Despite their openness, the ugly, unkind rumors began to spread. "How can a man and woman spend so much time together and *just* be friends?" "They are both married--how can they flaunt their relationship like that?" Eventually Kevin and Claire had to cool their friendship due to rumors and some discrete pressure from the college administration, thus ending the non-affair of Kevin and Claire.

The problem of Kevin and Claire is not new because male and female friends are often the subject of close scrutiny and skepticism. Many people seem to believe that opposite sex friends cannot spend time together without getting sexually involved. Is this really the case, though? Is it not possible for males and females to be "just" friends? This is one of the questions I will try to answer in this chapter, but before I can do so, I must first explain the love of friendship.

FRIENDSHIP DEFINED

Friendship is the most flexible relationship we will ever experience. The term 'friend' covers a broad range of relationships, from our very limited acquaintance with the teller at the bank to people we have known since childhood into our adult life. Consequently, friendship is the most difficult love to define. The best way to define this elusive love is to start with the obvious and work our way up to the not so obvious. I will begin with a few self-evident observations about friendship, then discuss the difference between best friends and lovers. Finally, I will end with a discussion about male/female friendships. To begin, here is my attempt at defining the distinguishing characteristic of friendship love:

FRIENDSHIP: a love characterized by equal regard[4] with respectful distance.

Let us take a closer look at this definition a phrase at a time.

Equal Regard. When I was in high school my campus was overflowing with students. The school had been designed for only 3,000 students and we had 4,500. Being rather shy, I had a difficult time making friends in such a big place. I eventually found my niche in the group of 200 plus musicians who made up the marching band.

In marching band I experienced friendship in a powerful way. The group had two important things in common: a love of music and a willingness to work hard. In the fall we practiced several hours a day learning the music and routines for the next football game. Because we all needed to work together to make each halftime performance succeed, there was a strong sense of camaraderie between the band members. It was because of my friendships in marching band that I finally overcame my shyness and began to reach out to other people.

My experience in marching band illustrates some of the characteristics of friendship. One characteristic of friendship is that we choose our friends. We usually pick people with whom we have something in common.[5] The commonalities might be work, religion, hobbies, or athletic pursuits. In my example of marching band, our love of music was one of the bonds we all had in common.

Having something in common with our friends implies another important trait of friendship: respect. Because we worked hard together, the band members respected each other. You cannot move a team of 200 plus people up and down a field unless they can get along. Though there are exceptions, we generally pick people whom we respect as equals to be our friends.[6] Lifestyle, social status, values, politics, and religion are often factors that determine whether or not we feel a person is our equal.

Combining the traits of something in common along with considering friends our equals, we have one half of the definition of friendship, equal regard. But there is more to friendship than just equal regard.

With Respectful Distance. At various times I worked in retail department stores. The hours were long and the pay was not great, but what made it bearable was the people with whom I worked. I could not help but get to know the life stories of those with whom I worked. There were students working between semesters, single parents getting by as best they could and people providing a second income for their families. The ups and downs of each person's life became a topic for much of our conversations. Yet at the end of our shifts, most of us went our separate ways after work. Some of us would occasionally get together but not very often. While we were close at work, there was an unspoken distance between many of us. We knew we could discuss our personal lives with each other at the store because we did not see each other away from the store. This is an example of the other side of friendship, respectful distance. We have equal regard for each other, we are close, but not so close that our lives and plans depend on each other.

The sense of connectedness, the level of commitment is distinctly less with friends than it is with family or romantic partners. We do not feel as great an obligation to rush to the aid of friends as we would for a spouse or lover. While we certainly feel some concern and obligation to assist friends, we are not as involved with the everyday details of their lives as we are with family or romantic partners. Rarely do friends depend upon each other for physical, emotional, and financial survival as you would with a spouse, lover, or family member.

A friendship may last a matter of weeks, months, or years. Friendships of varying length go in and out of our lives on a regular basis. Usually we are not very disturbed by such transiency, we sense this is normal for the large majority of our friends.

BEST FRIENDS

While "equal regard with respectful distance" may describe our more transitory friendships, there is one aspect of friendship it does not include. My definition does not account for the special experience of having a 'best' friend. To complete the definition I must add one more phrase.

FRIENDSHIP: a love characterized by equal regard with respectful distance, augmented by kindness and solicitude.

Kindness, a gentle caring for others, is a trait I have found in all of the different loves. I draw attention to it under friendship because, intuitively at least, friendship seems to be the simplest or most basic of all the loves. While kindness is a quality of many friendships, it is a particularly important trait of best friends. I pick my best friends, in part, on the basis of how they treat me, and kindness is high on the list. But even more than kindness, solicitude is the most distinguishing feature of best friendships as opposed to friendships in general. I care enough about my best friends, and they about me, to be solicitous, or have a lively concern, about each other's well-being. A best friend is someone I can turn to in a crisis, when I am making important decisions, or want someone around for no particular reason. And if my best friends have similar needs, they can turn to me for help or general companionship.

CAN LOVERS BE BEST FRIENDS?

Many people describe their romantic partners their best friends. Is it possible for romantic partners to be best friends? My own feeling is no. To demand that our lover have the objectivity and detachment of a best friend is an impossible expectation to lay upon them.[7] When I say that lovers cannot be best friends, I am presuming there is a difference between best friends and lovers. What is the difference between the two? The characteristic that distinguishes best friends from lovers can be summed up in one word: availability.[8]

We simply do not make ourselves as available to our best friends as we do to our own romantic partners. Consider the case of Kevin and Claire. Despite appearances and rumors, the level of availability between them was limited. Kevin and Claire spent a lot of time with each other on campus during work hours, but hardly saw each other off campus. They spent most of their time away from work with their families. Kevin & Claire illustrate the difference between best friends and lovers. We do not depend on our best friends for emotional, physical, and financial survival on a daily basis. Because we do not depend upon our best friends as much as we depend on our lovers, our best friends can give us a more objective viewpoint. We can radically differ with our best friends on such things as religion, politics, and values and still remain friends. Lovers have a hard time being objective about differences because they depend on each other for so much. The differences could be something as simple as the color of the bathroom curtains, or as complex as religion. Since we have chosen to intertwine our life, hopes, and goals with another human in romantic love, all that we say, do, and believe affects one another greatly. Because of the difference in availability between best friends and romantic partners, it is unrealistic to expect lovers to also be best friends.

Many people disagree with the idea that lovers cannot be best friends. Perhaps another way of looking at the question will clarify things. Hugh Prather comments that many people are searching for the perfect mate, but seem unable to find them. The reason so many people cannot find the perfect mate is that they have confused expectations about friends and lovers. The vision of a perfect mate that so many of us have is really a composite of several good friends we have had in the past.[9] While Prather was mainly addressing the important point that one person can never completely meet the needs of another, I think he also has something to say about best friends and lovers. We will always have the need for friends, whether we have a romantic partner or not. To expect our lover to be a substitute for our friends is unhealthy and unrealistic. We will always have the need to talk to and be with people without having to worry about their reaction to us. This breathing space we all need is uniquely filled by the friendships we have cultivated. As we will always need and have a lover, we will always need and have our friends. A succinct way of saying this is that while lovers can be friends, friends cannot be lovers.

MALE/FEMALE FRIENDSHIPS

Male/female friendship seems to be a lost art in our culture. The case of Kevin and Claire is a perfect example. Here are two adults who did all they could to dispel rumors and wrong impressions. Despite their best efforts, the college community had no concept of male/female friendships, so by default their friendship "had to be" an illicit sexual relationship.

Why is it so hard to develop male/female friendships? Part of the problem is that jealousy rears its ugly head in friendships with members of the opposite sex. Our romantic partners fear they may be replaced by our friends of the opposite sex. Since jealousy is such an enduring problem I have devoted an entire chapter to it (Chapter Six). For now I will focus on another aspect of male/female friendships.

We males tend to view women in predominantly sexual terms because we are prisoners of the "ideology of romantic love."[10] Many of us grew up with the expectation of finding that one special person with whom we would fall in love and live with happily ever after. Love, sex, passion, and happiness are all rolled into one great vision. The result is that many (most?) of us males approach females with the mind set of "I wonder what kind of romantic partner she would be." This mind set creates enormous problems about intimacy between the sexes. When we are used to equating love, sex, and happiness, it seems almost impossible to imagine men and women being intimate without being sexually involved. Is it possible for men and women to be intimate without being sexually involved? My answer is a resounding *yes,* depending on what you mean by intimacy.

INTIMACY DEFINED

Intimacy is the ability to share your fears, pains, hopes, and joys with others and to receive the same from others. Defined this way, intimacy does not require sexual involvement. While sex can add to intimacy, it is not a prerequisite for it. Returning to our example of Claire and Kevin, we can see why their community had problems with their friendship. Being heavily influenced by the ideology of romantic love, any kind of intimacy between males and females was viewed as sexual intimacy. Claire and Kevin were intimate as I have defined it, but not sexually intimate. It was the possibility of men and women being intimate without being sexual that their community refused to accept.

Intimacy is difficult for many people to achieve. Like any skill, intimacy is something that we must learn. Ideally, we would learn the skill of intimacy in our family upbringing.

Unfortunately, the family upbringing of many people has only made it harder for them to be intimate with others. So where do we learn intimacy? Many of us will learn how to be intimate in the friendships we develop.

Friendship is a foundational love for many, being the gateway to the intimacy found in the other loves. The relational skills of equal regard with respectful distance, kindness, solicitude, and intimacy we learn in our friendships will carry over into our other relationships. Explaining the relational skills of friendship is beyond the scope of this book. Fortunately, there are many good books available for those who wish to learn.[11]

MALE/FEMALE FRIENDS: WHAT ABOUT SEXUAL ATTRACTION?

Using the definition of intimacy I have given here, it is possible for men and women to be intimate without being sexually involved. But what do we do about the sexual dimension of male/female relationships? It does not disappear simply by definition. My own experience has been that sexual attraction is never completely absent from male/female friendships. To feel some attraction is normal, for it is the way we are wired physically and emotionally. A person's attractiveness may even influence our choice of him or her as a friend. Still, there may be some feeling of discomfort at being sexually attracted to someone of the opposite sex who is "just a friend." What do we do?

The first thought might be to discuss the issue of attraction between friends of the opposite sex. I am not so sure this really accomplishes anything, however. Most people will feel awkward, even threatened by a frank expression of sexual feelings. Depending on the level of openness in the friendship, the topic of mutual sexual attraction may never be discussed at all. In my own experience, the issue was not discussed with most of my female friends, and I do not think the friendships suffered because of it. Given our culture's obsession with sex, it has actually been a wonderful relief to be close to members of the opposite sex and not have to worry about dealing with the problem of "should we or shouldn't we?" As friends, the issue was not an option to discuss or act out. Yet the question of sexual attraction between friends of the opposite sex will continue to be a struggle to deal with. There is a way to overcome the struggle and uncertainty; for lack of a better term I call it 'spiritual growth.'

15

RELIGION AND SPIRITUAL GROWTH

While we cannot overlook the differences between them, there is at least one point at which several major religions seem to converge. They talk about our need to discipline our passions or desires. The Taoists call it "scheming ambition,"[12] the Buddhists call it "craving desire,"[13] the Christians call it "deceitful lust."[14] The popular impression of these religions' talk of disciplining our passions is that they are out to spoil our fun. People often think that these religious traditions believe the body is evil, sexuality is to be avoided, and emotions should be tuned out. Both Taoism and Buddhism have strong ascetical traditions, as does Christianity. And no doubt you will find such anti-body, anti-sex, and anti-emotion strands of belief in each tradition. But all three religions have a great number of sects, and not all of them are so negative about our bodies, sexuality, or emotions. In what I consider the healthier versions of each religion, the primary reasons for disciplining our passions are roughly the same. The Taoist seeks to curb his or her scheming ambition in order to draw closer to Tao, the organizing principle of the universe, and to avoid creating enmity in relationships with other people. The Buddhist seeks to control his or her craving desire in order to break out of the cycle of pain and suffering so many people endure in this life, and to prepare for Nirvana, a state where all desire is extinguished.[15] The Christian seeks to control his or her deceitful lusts in order to draw closer to God, and to achieve more loving relationships with other people. In each of these traditions a major goal or consequence of disciplining one's desires is an improved quality of relationship with other human beings. The improvement in the quality of relationships most certainly includes friendships, and in particular can include male/female friendships.

Just how does spiritual growth help the quality of male/female friendships? By giving us the strength to choose between letting our hormones control us, or we controlling our hormones. Unless we learn a little self discipline of our desires, male/female friendships will remain a rare occurrence. Unfortunately, sheer will power is not enough to keep our passions under control. As to how spiritual growth enables us to rise above our passions, I will leave that discussion for the chapter on spiritual love.

We have come a long way in this chapter. We started with friendship in general, working our way to best friends, to lovers and friends, and finally to male/female friends. We have touched upon the need for spiritual growth in building the kind of friendship that is possible between men and women. Looking ahead, we will also find that spiritual growth can also help improve the quality of the other loves in addition to friendship. But first we must discuss what is perhaps the best known of all the loves, romantic love. It is to romantic love that we now turn in the next chapter.

CHAPTER THREE

ROMANTIC LOVE

"We must first learn how we are like other people before we learn how we are different."

Cheryl and Peter had both endured their share of painful relationships. Cheryl left her boyfriend of several years when he would not deal with his alcoholism. Peter divorced his wife of eight years when she refused to deal with the abuse she suffered in childhood. Cheryl and Peter had each gambled in intimacy and had come out on the losing end.

Cheryl and Peter had both avoided serious relationships for several years. Cheryl worked on her co-dependency that had lead her to the no-win relationship with her last boyfriend. Peter worked on his low self-esteem that had led him to endure years of angry put downs and verbal tirades of his ex-wife. Neither Cheryl nor Peter felt much hope of finding a truly intimate relationship. When they met each other for the first time, all of the hopelessness about intimacy disappeared.

Cheryl and Peter first met on a bike hike organized by mutual friends. They ended up riding together and hit it off right away. After discussing the usual topics of jobs and interests, the conversation quickly moved to more serious topics. When they each shared about their past relationships and healing processes, they sensed in each other a kindred spirit, someone in whom they could trust and confide. At first they started seeing each other as friends, but they quickly fell in love and started dating.

Their first two months in love were "heaven on earth" according to Cheryl. They spent a lot of time together dancing, going to movies and, of course, biking. Both felt as if they had known each other forever, although they had only been together a few weeks. Eventually the heaven on earth feeling began to fade from their relationship. After about three months together, they saw each other's imperfections and insecurities more clearly. As their disillusionment with each other increased, their fights became more frequent and vicious. Cheryl was afraid of losing Peter and began going out of her way to please him. She lost touch with her friends and let personal interests slide. For his part, Peter was beginning to withdraw from Cheryl. Being a person who kept mostly to himself, he never had many friends. Peter felt smothered by Cheryl's constant attention and started to find more reasons to be busy and unable to see her.

At six months into their relationship Cheryl and Peter were close to calling it quits. Cheryl was convinced that Peter did not love her enough and was deliberately ignoring her. Peter was convinced that Cheryl was trying to control him and felt she was too possessive and jealous of him. They decided to go and see a counselor before giving up on each other.

The experience of Peter and Cheryl reflects that of many people. At first love begins in a wonderful rush of emotion. Eventually the ecstasy wears off and each partner sees that their lover is not as perfect as they had thought. Arguments happen more frequently and dissatisfaction mounts. Should they quit or tough it out? Should they take what they can get or move on in hope of finding a better, more perfect relationship? Before any couple can answer these questions, they

20

must be able to answer a more basic question: What is romantic love?

ROMANTIC LOVE DEFINED

ROMANCE: A love characterized by a sense of emotional balance and a strong sexual attraction that gives the partners an overall feeling of completion in their relationship with each other.

Let us take a closer look at this definition.

A Sense of Emotional Balance. In *Symposium*, Plato's ancient dialogue on love, the Greek humorist Aristophanes offers a frivolous explanation for the intensity of love. Originally, we humans were spherical creatures with four arms and four legs. We were a very prideful race, thinking very highly of ourselves. Such unbridled egotism was noticed by the gods, in particular by Zeus, head honcho on Mount Olympus. Zeus took offense at the humans' prideful ways and decided to do something about it. He split those original humans in two so that each became thin, frail beings of two arms and two legs. The original unity of each human was torn asunder as Zeus scattered the various halves of humanity all over the world. Thus we became two legged, two armed creatures doomed to wander the earth seeking the other half of ourselves.

While we may smile at the crude mythology of Aristophanes, his story does illustrate an enduring belief about romantic love: we find a sense of emotional balance or completion in our romantic partner.[16] Carl Jung incorporated this idea into his psychological theories. Jung argued that we are attracted to people who have developed aspects of their personality that we have not developed. Very few of us have fully developed the four basic parts of human personality of bodily sense, intuition, thinking and feeling. Most of us excel in one of the four parts of human personality. For example, people with well developed thinking abilities might go into the sciences for a career. Someone with a highly developed sense of intuition might pursue work in the arts or humanities. A person with a keen sense of body might embark on a career in athletics. What romantic love can provide is a sense of emotional balance for us by our choosing someone who compliments our less developed abilities.

As a physics major in college I had a well developed thinking ability. Like most thinking types, the least developed part of my personality was my feelings. I was uncomfortable discussing my feelings with other people and even hid from my own feelings. In my social life I tended to become

21

involved with women who were gifted in the arts, such as music, or the human sciences, such as psychology. These gifted women taught me to become more aware of my own feelings. It was their deep awareness of their own feelings that balanced my own lack of awareness. Eventually I became comfortable enough with my own feelings to pursue work in the humanities instead of the sciences. If I had not learned more about myself from the women I was romantically involved with, I would not have pursued a career in the humanities. The sense of emotional balance that comes from romantic love can have life changing affects upon us all.

A Strong Sexual Attraction. Perhaps the most widely accepted feature of romantic love is the eternal attraction between the opposite sexes. The exhilaration of first meeting, the continuing sense of energy, even mystery, are all part of the love that two people share with each other. The sense of emotional balance has its counterpart in the physical union of man and woman. While sexual attraction is an important feature of romantic love, it is not the most distinguishing feature of romantic love.

It is all too easy to mistake the passion of falling in love with love itself. For many couples, sexual intimacy may be part of the first few weeks of their new relationship. Sexual intimacy can enhance the sense of newness, the excitement of discovering someone whom you can love and who returns that love in kind. But there is a hazard to thinking that falling in love and sexual attraction are all there is to romantic love. Eventually the intensity of the initial passion will fade. After a few weeks or months, two lovers become familiar with each other. When the passion fades and sex is no longer as explosive, does this mean love is over and done? If passionate feelings and explosive sex are all that constitute romantic love, then yes the love is over when the excitement dies down.

Have you ever found yourself in a relationship where the passion is gone? You start to think "There must be something more!" The shortcomings of your lover become more obvious and then the endless nitpicking begins. "He isn't as tall as I would like." "She isn't as pretty as I would like." "He doesn't make as much money as I want." "She is not as educated as I would like." Eventually the relationship ends and we are back to square one. We start playing the dating game, hoping to find someone to fall in love with all over again. But is this really the way to find lasting love? We fall in love, we fall out of love, and then the cycle begins again... and again ...and again. This is the dilemma facing Peter and Cheryl six months into their relationship. They still love each other but they are both frustrated. Cheryl feels she is not getting enough attention and Peter feels he is giving too much. The temptation to move on and find a "better" love is strong for both of them, but

22

chances are they would end up in the same place again.

How do people like Cheryl and Peter avoid the cycle of falling into and out of love? By realizing that falling in love is not the same as being in love. Before we can appreciate the difference between falling in love and being in love, we must first complete the definition of romantic love. If sexual attraction and the passion of falling in love are not the heart and soul of romantic love, what is?

Gives the Partners an Overall Feeling of Completion in Their Relationship with Each Other. What is it that we find 'completed' with our romantic partner? What does a sense of emotional balance and strong sexual attraction tell us we find in our lover that we cannot find alone? What we find with our romantic partner is a complete sense of self. "It is shared selfhood that defines [romantic] love" as Robert Solomon puts it.[17] A sense of shared selfhood that two people create in love is the defining characteristic of romantic love. What does it mean that we are creating a shared selfhood with our romantic partner? It means that we do not create the unique personalities we are apart from other people.

LOVE AND THE INDIVIDUAL?

Our culture has a strong tradition of exalting the individual. From the seventeenth and eighteenth century Enlightenment philosophies to modern therapy there has been a steady emphasis upon the isolated individual. Whether it is religious and political beliefs or the kind of clothes we wear, all such things are supposedly decided by us apart from the influence of others. But is that really the case?

> What reason tells us--most unreasonably--is that we are each self-contained, self-defining individuals. Our philosophies assume this. Our individualist pride endorses it. Our therapies confirm it. The truth is, however, that the self is a social construct, mutually defined with and through other people. And if this is so, love is not a mysterious 'union' of two otherwise separate and isolated selves but rather a special instance of the mutually defined creation of selves.[18]

We are not the complete, self-contained individuals that many of our cultural traditions would

23

have us believe. We learn who we are only in relationship to other people.

The relentless pursuit of romantic love by so many people now begins to make sense. Many of us have fallen for the belief that we are complete, self-contained individuals. But deep down we also sense that something is wrong with our exaltation of the individual. Maybe we sense that romantic love provides an important corrective to excessive individualism.

I have learned that I feel incomplete unless I am able to share experiences with other people. Sometimes I take trips into the mountains alone. On one winter trip I skied into a remote mountain valley. After much effort I made it to a promontory that gave me a panorama of the whole valley. I found a wonderful solitude on that promontory. It was just me, the blue sky, snow covered mountains and a gentle wind. As exhilarating as it was to be up there alone, I did not keep quiet about my adventure. My trip to the mountains was not a part of my personal history until I told someone about it. I think this is also true about other parts of our lives. Whether we are trying to figure out what we believe or just struggling to get through another day, we cannot sort these things out unless we share them with others. Romantic love gives us a chance to share with one special person, to create together a sense of self that we cannot create alone.

Peter and Cheryl had each done a lot emotional growth on their own, but you can only go so far on your own in developing a full sense of self. When Cheryl and Peter first met they sensed a balance in each other's presence that they lacked on their own. To complete their respective senses of self they needed to be in relationship with each other. The problems they are running into involve knowing how to negotiate and put together this shared self they are creating with each other. What Peter and Cheryl are experiencing is the difficult transition from falling in love to being in love.

FALLING IN LOVE & BEING IN LOVE

Many arguments have been made for and against the experience of falling in love. Some hold that falling in love is nothing more than a regression to unfulfilled childhood fantasies and wishes. Others argue that the excitement and thrill of falling in love is the essence of romantic love. The best approach I have seen is somewhere in the middle. Falling in love is a real and genuine experience but it is not infallible, nor is falling in love to be confused with being in love.[19]

Falling in love or love at first sight has been experienced by many people. We meet someone for the first time or see an old acquaintance in a new, passionate way, and suddenly we are obsessed with the romantic possibilities with this person. The experience of falling in love is basically one of fantasizing about our potential romantic partner. While sexual desire will be a part of it, a good portion of our fantasizing is projecting what it would be like to be in relationship with our potential romantic partner. We imagine what it would be like to create a shared selfhood with our potential lover, such as talking and spending time together.

Cheryl and Peter had experienced falling in love before. In each of their previous relationships they had fallen in love, thinking they had found long term romantic partners. Unfortunately for both of them, their intuitions of falling in love had proven to be painfully mistaken. But when Cheryl and Peter met each other, their intuition of falling in love proved to be more accurate. All of this points to the difficult truth that the experience of falling in love is not infallible.

What is it that sets off the experience of falling in love? The trigger for the experience varies from person to person. It might be the color of one's eyes, the style of hair, physical build, or just the name of the person concerned. Falling in love does not happen in a vacuum, for each of us has been preparing for our 'ideal' lover in our imagination for years. Movies, stories, songs, others we have known and admired all contribute to our personal image of our lover-to-be. Part of the rush of falling in love must come from these latent expectations we have been building for so long.

While I believe falling in love is a real experience, there is a down side to it. We have to be honest with ourselves and admit that very often our intuitions about possible romantic partners are terribly mistaken. The real person we fell in love with may be vastly different from what we expected. They may not be in a position to return our love due to another relationship or other circumstances. And most painful of all, they may not even have the slightest interest in us as a possible romantic partner. The best way to approach falling in love is to view it as a way our intuition tells us that here is someone who <u>could</u> become a romantic partner. Romantic love will not automatically develop all by itself. To move from the passionate frenzy of falling in love to being in love takes time and work.

When the excitement of falling in love settles down, the next step is to move from falling in love to being in love. A major snag in Cheryl and Peter's relationship is this difficult transition from falling in love to being in love. At about three months into their relationship the original rush of falling in love had faded. They began to see each other's imperfections and to fight about them. It is here in making the transition from falling in love to being in love that the definition and criteria

25

of love in general comes into play. Peter and Cheryl were doubting the reality of their love because of the problems and arguments. But if we consider the definition and criteria of love in general, we can see that they are still very much in love. In seeing a counselor together, Cheryl and Peter are demonstrating commitment and responsibility. When things got tough they both remained committed to their relationship instead of quitting. Seeking professional help for their problems shows that they accept responsibility for finding solutions to their problems. They remain vulnerable to each other by discussing their frustrations and difficulties. Peter and Cheryl have been reverting to old patterns of behavior from previous unhealthy relationships. Now they want to find new patterns of behaving for their new relationship. Peter and Cheryl want to be new and better people with each other, to grow beyond their old, inadequate selves of the past. While they are having problems, they still feel enough safety and sanctuary to discuss their problems with each other. Being caught between old behaviors of the past and not knowing how to implement healthier behavior leaves open the question of whether their relationship was based on need or love. One of the goals in therapy will undoubtedly be to move their relationship away from a need basis to love instead.

CONFUSING LOVE WITH THE RELATIONSHIP

Cheryl and Peter's struggle with old behavior patterns from previous relationships raises an important question. Is the relationship we have with our partner the same as the love we have for our partner? This may seem like splitting hairs, but the distinction between love and the relationship has important consequences. Robert Solomon argues that our relationship is *not* the same as our love for our partner.[20] How can this be? Consider the examples of unrequited love and the love one has for a deceased partner. In unrequited love, one person has developed love for another person without the other person knowing about or responding to that love. The emotion of love exists in one person for another yet without any established two way relationship with the beloved. In the case of love for a deceased partner, the emotion of love continues to exist even when there is no longer a relationship of any kind. Both examples point to the idea that the love we have for someone is not quite the same as our relationship with them.

What do I mean by relationship? A working definition of relationship could be "a set of negotiated behavior patterns directed toward a particular goal." This covers a wide variety of possible relationships, from the transitory ritual of buying something at the checkout stand to establishing a home and marriage to raise a family. The goals range from who takes out the garbage to financial and living arrangements for a whole family. The word 'negotiate' is a bit slippery, for there are goals that are 'negotiated' in love-relationships about which we may not be fully aware. Some of the goals and behavior patterns may be dictated by subconscious or dysfunctional problems. Examples would be an enabler looking for an alcoholic personality to 'help' in a relationship, or a victim of child abuse looking for a lover to fill the role of an abusive parent. These examples of negotiating unhealthy behavior patterns to achieve less than beneficial goals brings us to the main reason for distinguishing between love and relationships.

What goals do Peter and Cheryl need to renegotiate in their relationship by going to a counselor? They want to renegotiate their behavior patterns to restore the unique characteristics of romantic love to their relationship: a sense of emotional balance and a feeling of completion. As we have already seen, Peter and Cheryl have not fallen out of love with each other. What is happening instead is that the balance or stability of their relationship is out of kilter. Old fears from previous relationships are keeping Peter and Cheryl from being intimate with each other. Cheryl is smothering Peter with her affection in fear of losing him and Peter is withdrawing to protect himself from being controlled and hurt by Cheryl. Peter and Cheryl have fallen into what Dean C. Delis calls the "passion paradox."[21]

THE PASSION PARADOX

When a relationship starts to move from falling in love to being in love, a problem often develops. One of the two partners seems to be more in love than the other. If the imbalance continues, the whole relationship can be thrown into jeopardy. The partner who is 'more' in love accuses the other of being insensitive, uncaring, and so on. The 'less' loving partner begins to withdraw and accuses the 'more' loving partner of being possessive, jealous, smothering, and so on. Arguments may develop and escalate, leaving the 'less' loving partner feeling guilty and the 'more' loving partner feeling abandoned. The situation feeds on itself and gets progressively worse. The passion paradox is that both partners naturally engage in behavior that only makes the situation worse. To escape the passion paradox they need to behave in a way that is just the opposite of what they have been doing.

Delis calls the person who 'loves too much' the "one down"[22] and the one who 'loves too little' the "one-up."[23] The one down (Cheryl in our example) is usually afraid of losing the relationship and exhibits jealousy and possessiveness in their behavior. The one-up (Peter in our example) often feels guilty of not loving enough, and exhibits aloof and withdrawn behavior toward the one down. Delis suggests different behavior strategies for the one-up and the one down to help restore balance to the relationship. For the one down he suggests "healthy distance."[24] A good way a one-down can avoid self-defeating possessiveness and jealousy is to stop putting all of their energy into the relationship. Instead they redirect their energy towards other hobbies and friendships in addition to the love-relationship so that the one-down's self-esteem is not entirely dependent on one person. For the one-up, Delis suggests "trial closeness"[25] with the one down. Being aloof and withdrawn from the one down only drives the one down to more possessive behavior. If the one-up makes time to be with the one down and shares their feelings, this will give the one down some reassurance.

Peter and Cheryl have fallen into the passion paradox. Cheryl feels she is giving too much and Peter is not giving enough. Peter is feeling smothered by Cheryl's attention and accuses her of being jealous and possessive. The natural tendencies of Cheryl to give too much and Peter to withdraw are simply aggravating the situation. Their frustration is continuing to build and things are getting worse. Cheryl needs to practice healthy distance by reclaiming her friends and personal interests she has been ignoring. Peter needs to practice trial closeness by spending more time with Cheryl and sharing his feelings more instead of withdrawing. By engaging in behaviors that are the opposite of what they have been doing, Cheryl and Peter will restore the sense of emotional balance and completion to their romantic love.

Healthy distance and trial closeness sound awfully familiar. Is this not friendship by another name? In the last chapter we saw that the difference between friendship and romantic love is the level of availability between people in the two loves. We make ourselves more available emotionally and physically to our lover than to our friends. And we find more objectivity with our friends because we are not as emotionally dependent on them as we are with our lover. The contribution that friendship makes to the longevity of romantic love is that we have learned that delicate balance between distance and closeness. At times a romantic relationship will need breathing room. If friendship is a part of romantic love, the two partners will realize the need to give each other some distance. They will understand that lovers can be close and intimate without being passionate and sexual all of the time. What Peter and Cheryl need to do is to relearn the art of friendship. They falsely believe the only way to be intimate is through intense romantic passion. Now that the passion has faded they do not know how to behave, and they have fallen into the passion paradox by relying on unhealthy behavior patterns from previous relationships. When the love of friendship is practiced in conjunction with romantic love, friendship will help sustain romantic love over the years.

If the question 'what is love?' is at the top of the list for this book, the second question would have to be 'how do you make love last, particularly romantic love?' We have already discussed how friendship helps to sustain romantic love. Another way to help romantic love last is working out shared dreams about the future.[26] When two people develop a personal history with each other this adds to the uniqueness of their relationship. Working out shared dreams for the future also adds to their sense of purpose in being together. It could be something as simple as a vacation cruise or the daunting task of raising children. The common dreams two people work to make come true give them both something to live for and look forward to in the years ahead.

The last suggestion I have for helping to keep love alive is the most intriguing of all. It is laughter.

It is, in a phrase, a mutual sense of humor. It is the ability to be *amused* by each other, to find faults as charms--often so easy in the first weeks of an affair but so soon infuriating when the efficiency demands of a relationship begin. It's hard to fall out of love as long as you are laughing together.[27]

I cannot think of a more positive thought on which to end this chapter: Love strongly, love deeply, and don't forget to laugh.

CHAPTER FOUR

SPIRITUAL LOVE

"For it is not what you are or have been that God looks at with this merciful eyes, but what you would be."

Larry and Beth were in love. They were engaged to be married after Larry finished college. Beth was a traditional woman, expecting Larry to support her financially while she stayed at home caring for their children. Everyone assumed Larry would work for Beth's father in real estate after college. Larry went along will all the plans people had for him because he did not know what else to do. Larry was never much of a planner, drifting through life, waiting for things to happen. Everything changed when Larry was almost killed in an accident.

Late one night, Larry was driving in a blizzard. It was difficult to see the car in front of him. Suddenly a blinding light, a loud noise brought pain and then darkness.

A large truck coming from the opposite direction had lost control on the icy road. It slid into Larry's lane of traffic, smashing the car in front of him before plowing into Larry. The truck driver survived the crash with minor injuries. Larry was hospitalized for weeks with a fractured leg, but the driver of the other car was not so lucky. She died instantly when her car was struck in the head on crash.

The tragedy received a lot of media attention since the young woman was a single mother of two small children. She had been well liked by neighbors and friends. All this weighed on Larry's mind and heart. While lying in the hospital, he had plenty of time to reflect. "Why was I spared and this woman allowed to die? She had more reason to live than me."

Larry had never been religious, but now he sensed a spiritual hunger. He needed to know why *his* life had been spared. He needed to feel that life was more than something that just happened to him.

Larry began to read all he could find on religion and philosophy. He tried to talk to Beth about his questions and studies, but she wasn't interested. When he said he was taking time off from school, she became scared. She said tragedies happen, it wasn't his fault the young mother had died. Beth said he needed to get on with life so they could marry and start their own family.

Larry could not be consoled. He dropped out of college and broke his engagement to Beth, saying he needed time to find some answers. Marrying her was impossible until he found those answers.

Larry spent the next few years traveling the world. He went to India and studied with some Hindu religious philosophers but came away unsatisfied. Larry went on to Japan and studied with Buddhist teachers. Again, he was unsatisfied. He found no answers to his questions: Why had his life been spared? Was life more than something that just happened to him?

Larry eventually returned to his hometown. He lived with his parents and worked at odd jobs. He went from one relationship to another. He would meet an interesting woman and become involved. He tried to explain his spiritual hunger, tried to talk about his studies and years abroad. Each woman listened politely but did not understand. Eventually, bored, Larry moved on to yet another relationship.

One day Larry woke to a shocking realization. He stared in the mirror that morning, studied his graying, receding hair, the wrinkles around his eyes. He was 40 years old, alone, and still did not have answers to his questions. Why was his life spared? Is life more than something that just happens to him?

Larry's story could be anyone's story. We feel a certain need for meaning in our lives, a sense of assurance that we have a purpose here. Some try to find answers in books. Others, perhaps most, seek meaning in romantic love. As helpful as these may be, that vague, nagging hunger for reassurance still remains. What are we seeking? The same thing Larry sought but could not find: spiritual meaning and reassurance. More accurately, it is a spiritual kind of love that he sought. It is a love that not only satisfies our spirit and mind but also satisfies our emotions in some paradoxical way. Naturally we seek to find this love within our romantic relationships, but somehow it remains elusive. There is a reason Larry and others cannot find this spiritual love in their romantic relationships. It is a love that is distinct from romantic love. It may be found within or as a part of romantic love, but romantic love is no substitute. The New Testament writers and later theologians called this spiritual love.

SPIRITUAL LOVE DEFINED

Spiritual love is usually explained in doctrinal or circular terms: "spiritual love is the love of God in Christ." "Spiritual love is the love exemplified in the life of Christ." For our purpose exploring the six loves we need a more straight forward definition of spiritual love.

Spiritual love: a love characterized by active compassion that seeks to enhance the spiritual transformation of others and oneself.[28]

Let us take a closer look at this definition, phrase by phrase.

Compassion. Compassion is the ability to step outside of our own personal needs and feelings, and experience the needs and feelings of others. We all do this to some extent already. Whenever a family member or friend comes to us with a problem, we instinctively forget ourselves for the moment, we "project" ourselves into their experience as we listen to them. Spiritual love demands more than compassion for the ones we love, however, for it is a love that is universal in its demand. To be compassionate to those we do not love or even know is something we must learn.

Active Compassion. The compassion of spiritual love is active, which is different from mere empathy. When we experience empathy, we feel pain in response to the suffering of others, but we are not moved to do anything about it. As an example, consider the emergency relief groups who show pictures on TV of starving children in order to help raise funds. A person who sees these pictures of suffering may feel genuine pain or guilt for a moment, but then they switch the channel to their favorite situation comedy. The viewer's empathy for the suffering children does not move them to take action for the children. In contrast, active compassion is moved to meet the needs of the people for whom it feels. Mother Teresa's work in India is a good example of active compassion. She felt for the dying people who had no place to go and was moved to give them a place in which they could die with dignity. Mother Teresa saw people in need and did something to meet that need. Her first little hospice has now turned into a worldwide order. Most people may not do anything as dramatic as Mother Teresa, but we can do something to help others in need. Active compassion may be as simple as sending a check to your favorite relief agency, or as complex as taking political action on behalf of those in need.

Spiritual Transformation. In the chapter on friendship we saw how three different mystical traditions converge on one point, the need to overcome our natural self-centeredness or egocentric need to control. Only when we address our egocentric need to control will male-female friendships become a common occurrence, but more is to be gained than the recovery of male-female friendships.

The primary goal of spiritual love is to overcome our self-centeredness so that the other loves can be expressed and enjoyed to their fullest extent. The fears and jealousies we harbor because of our need to control create problems in the other loves. The transformation of spiritual love helps liberate the other loves from our egocentric need to control. Spiritual love will not prevent problems in the other loves, but if we have worked on our need to control we will be in a better position to work through the problems of the other loves.

CONTEMPLATIVE PRAYER

Within the Christian faith, the mystical tradition is maintained and practiced in contemplative prayer. Contemplative prayer seeks to develop spiritual love and conquer our natural self-centeredness. Contemplation is a prayer of silence, a quiet listening in the presence of God. As much as possible, the mind is emptied of all thoughts, images, and chatter. While other forms of prayer are practiced, such as petitionary prayer and meditation on scripture, contemplation is considered the deepest form of prayer.

How exactly does this transformation of the egocentric need to control take place? A fourteenth century English mystic says it best. "For it is not what you are or have been that God looks at with his merciful eyes, but what you would be." The emphasis in contemplative prayer is not upon sins or misdeeds of the past. Although the past cannot be ignored, the emphasis is upon what we can become: more loving of ourselves and others.

There are several stages of spiritual growth that the contemplative passes through on the way to spiritual transformation. Usually the contemplative is assisted by a Spiritual Director, a fellow contemplative who has been practicing for several years. The Spiritual Director helps a student of contemplation understand the deep changes he or she will go through as they pass through the different stages of prayer. In the early stages we start to heal hurts from our past. We learn how our own fears and hopes are the same as everyone else's, which leads to the development of compassion for ourselves and others. In the later stages we learn what is unique about ourselves by achieving a more accurate self-image. An accurate self-image helps free us from our fears and jealousies that interfere with the other loves. I will have more to say on this process in the chapter on jealousy.

Through all of his years of study and travel, what Larry sought was a love that focuses on spiritual transformation. When he studied Hindu philosophy and Buddhist philosophy, he did so under the guidance of a Spiritual Director or teacher. Yet this was not enough, for Larry wanted something more personal in regard to his spiritual needs. He sought it in romantic love but failed to find it. What was he looking for?

Spiritual Love. Spiritual love does not just happen to us, but must be nurtured in relationships with people we know and trust. These relationships are with people who are specifically dedicated to the growth and practice of spiritual love. Larry sought this spiritual support in his romantic partners but could not find it. What was the problem?

WHY SPIRITUAL LOVE IS CONFUSED WITH ROMANTIC LOVE

Larry is confusing two important but distinct needs. Like all humans, Larry has a need for intimacy, to love and be loved by others. He naturally seeks to meet this need in romantic relationships. Larry is correct in trying to meet his basic need for human companionship in romantic love. But he is also searching for a relationship that was devoted to his spiritual needs. When Larry tried to force this on his spiritual needs on his romantic partner, he ended up losing the relationship.

Since spiritual love is a distinct love, it requires its own special relationship. Within the Christian faith the need for this special relationship has been met in a number of ways. Small prayer and Bible study groups are one way, and having a Spiritual Director to meet with regularly is another. Belonging to a church and developing relationships within the congregation is yet another. Whatever method is used, there is the specific goal of focusing on spiritual growth and the deepening of one's faith.

Are spiritual love and romantic love mutually exclusive? No, but to expect one person to fully engage in romantic love and spiritual love simultaneously is too much for anyone to satisfy. The needs that each love tries to meet are very different. Sharing one's needs and interests regarding spiritual growth are certainly an important part of sustaining romantic and marital love over time. But in developing relationships based on spiritual love there is a situation similar to that of friendship. Spiritual love involves an objectivity that is hard to reach in romantic or marital love, for spiritual transformation affects every aspect of a person's life. To expect one's romantic partner to be fully objective about such a total process is too unreasonable. Belonging to a group where spiritual love is the primary focus will meet one's spiritual needs without burdening their romantic partner too heavily. This takes pressure off of one's romantic partner and even strengthens the relationship in the long run. Just as there is a need for friendships in addition to a romantic or marriage relationship, there is a similar need for spiritual love relationships beyond romance or marriage.

Larry's fundamental mistake was to expect Beth and later romantic partners to satisfy both his needs for romance and spiritual love. If he had realized he was confusing the two loves perhaps his circumstances would have been different. Instead of being alone at age 40, he could have had a romantic relationship and a circle of people devoted to the practice of spiritual love, meeting both his romantic and spiritual needs. Beth could also have helped the situation more than she did. Had she been aware of her own spiritual needs, she might have been more sympathetic with the psychic pain that Larry was suffering. She could not have met all of his needs as he expected her to do, but the two of them could have found a group that met their need for spiritual love. If Larry and Beth had taken more responsibility for meeting their spiritual needs, perhaps Larry would not have left Beth.

As important as spiritual transformation is, it cannot take place in a vacuum. When a person lacks the basics of food, shelter, and clothing, they are not going to be concerned with spiritual growth. Here is where political and social responsibility become a part of spiritual love. If we are to enhance the spiritual growth of others, we must first create the conditions under which spiritual transformation will occur. If someone is starving, out of work, or homeless, they have little use for pious talk of spiritual love and spiritual transformation.

SPIRITUAL LOVE AND SOCIAL RESPONSIBILITY

How do we fit spiritual love together with social and political responsibility? By realizing that the practice of spiritual love occurs within a religious community, and that the nature of community involves more than meeting the needs of individuals. Spiritual love practiced within community carries with it an ethic of caring for those beyond the immediate religious community. How can this be illustrated? One illustration is found in the Old Testament prophetic tradition.

Isaiah 58 is a classic statement of the need for social and political responsibility in conjunction with religious observances. This passage answers, in part, the question of how spiritual love is related to social and political responsibility. Isaiah 58 offers an illustration of how the practice of prayer, worship and other observances is meant to do more than meet the needs of the individual members of the believing community.

In Isaiah 58, it seems that the faithful have been complaining to God that he does not hear their prayers. They have been meticulously following proper rituals in fasting, worship, and prayer. Yet, God does not respond to their prayers. Why does he not respond?

"Why have we fasted, and thou seest it not? Why have we humbled ourselves, and thou takest no knowledge of it?' (Isaiah 58:3, RSV)

Through the prophet Isaiah, God answers, saying that the faithful's following of ritual is worthless in his sight.

> Behold, in the day of your fast you seek your own pleasure, and oppress all your workers. Behold, you fast only to quarrel and to fight and to hit with wicked fist. Fasting like yours this day will not make your voice to be heard on high. (Isaiah 58:3-4, RSV)

The religious observances that God seeks are very different from what the faithful have been offering to Him.

> Is not this the fast I choose: to loose the bonds of wickedness, to undo the thongs of the yoke, to let the oppressed go free, and to break every yoke? Is it not to share your bread with the hungry, and bring the homeless poor into your house; when you see the naked, to cover him, and not to hide yourself from your own flesh? Then shall your light break forth like the dawn, and your healing shall spring up speedily; your righteousness shall go before you, the glory of the Lord shall be your rear guard. Then you shall call, and the Lord will answer; you shall cry, and he will say, Here I am. (Isaiah 58:6-8a, 9, RSV)

What we are seeing in this passage is the collision between two different visions of community. The unhappy faithful believe the purpose of religious community is to meet their own individual needs. They see no obligation to care for anyone beyond their own group. Isaiah is telling them that their vision of community is too limited and self-serving. The spiritual practices of prayer, fasting, worship and other observances should make us more mindful of those less fortunate than us. Even more, these practices should move us to do something to help our fellow humans in distress. How can these conflicting visions of religious community be reconciled? By realizing that spiritual love is inseparable from yet another form of spiritual love, a community based love or group from of love: community love. The vision or model on which religious community is based will determine the emphasis and practice of spiritual love. The unhappy faithful wanted to worry about only themselves, so their practice of spiritual love was limited to their own group. But Isaiah wants them to broaden their practice of spiritual love to include the poor and suffering beyond their own religious community. Why is Isaiah so adamant about connecting social action for the unfortunate to the spiritual practices of his religious community? Because a person's spiritual needs are inseparable from their physical and emotional needs. If the unhappy faithful had been more aware of this fact, perhaps they would have been more willing to help people beyond their own group.

The New Testament letter of James amplifies the idea that our spiritual and physical needs are inseparable. James writes that it makes no sense to worry about someone's spiritual needs if other needs are not being met.

> If a brother or sister is ill-clad and in lack of daily food, and one of you says to them, "Go in peace, be warmed and filled," without giving them the things needed for the body, what does it profit? So faith by itself, if it has no works, is dead. (Js 2:15-17, RSV)

Meeting the spiritual *and* physical needs of people is what James means by 'works' of faith. Like Isaiah, James sees active concern for the physical and spiritual needs of others as part of the purpose of religious community.

I will have more to say on community love in the next chapter. The point to remember for now is that the practice of spiritual love within a religious community carries with it an ethic or concern for people beyond one's immediate religious community. What does this say about political and social responsibility in relation to spiritual love? If we truly seek to enhance the spiritual transformation of others, we must create the conditions in which spiritual transformation can take place. This means taking action to feed the starving, clothe the naked and give shelter to the homeless. Those who would meet the spiritual needs of others by preaching the Gospel to them must first meet their basic needs, for the body and the spirit are inseparable. If we truly care about the spiritual welfare of our fellow humans, we must also care about their bodily needs. Thus there is implicit in spiritual love and community love a concern for social and political responsibility for meeting the physical and spiritual needs of our fellow humans. The practice of spiritual love and community love *without* social and political responsibility is nothing more than narcissism by another name.

Of Others and Oneself. The Lone Ranger approach to spirituality has no place within spiritual love. Spiritual love occurs between people in community with other people. Some people will hear a call to live a solitary life for God apart from the world in monasteries or cloisters, but their numbers will be small. Most of us will have to work out our salvation with others of our faith living in a secular world. Thus, at heart, spiritual love is a reciprocal love.[29] When we share this kind of love with another person we expect that love to be returned to us. To say that spiritual love is reciprocal goes against the belief of many Christians who think spiritual love is completely selfless. 'Selfless' usually means that when we love someone, we are totally concerned about the welfare of the one we love. We do not worry about our own needs, we do not expect any response to our love.

SPIRITUAL LOVE IS NOT SELFLESS

I do not agree with the selfless view of spiritual love because it goes against our experiences of loving other people. How many of us would remain in a friendship or romance where our loving concern was not reciprocated? How many of us would remain in a church where our practice of spiritual love was not returned in kind? Very few of us would remain in such circumstances. We have a need for love and to love, and to deny either side of that need is to deny ourselves in a destructive way. Viewed in this way, the old commandment to "Love your neighbor as yourself" may be practical advice as much as it is a religious command.

Are there circumstance under which spiritual love *does* become selfless? To answer that question, I will use the term 'self giving' instead of 'selfless.' So then the question becomes are there any circumstances in which spiritual love becomes self giving love? Yes, there are such circumstances. When I say self giving love I mean spiritual love that perseveres even when there is no hope of that love being reciprocated. An example of such self giving spiritual love is the Old Testament story of the prophet Hosea.

The Old Testament prophetic tradition portrays the relationship between God and the nation of Israel in many ways. One of the most moving metaphors is that of God as a devoted parent and Israel as a wayward child. In Hosea's time of 750 B.C., several centuries had passed since the Exodus from Egypt. After settling down to life in the Promised Land, it seems that the

Hebrews were losing interest in their God. So began the history of the Prophets sent to bring Israel back to its faith and its God. Hosea was one of the first Prophets called to speak to Israel on behalf of the Lord.

In the eleventh chapter of Hosea we see the metaphor of God as parent and Israel as the child. The intensity of that love comes across very powerfully.

> When Israel was a child, I loved him, and out of Egypt I called my son. The more I called them, the more they went from me; they kept sacrificing to Baals, and burning incense to idols. Yet it was I who taught Ephraim to walk, I took them up in my arms; but they did not know that I healed them. I led them with cords of compassion, with bands of love, and I became to them as one who eases the yoke on their jaws, and I bent down to them and fed them. (Hosea 11:1-4, RSV)

God took the initiative of reaching out to Israel and attempted to lead them in a growing faith, but there were problems. Like any child, the nation of Israel had a mind of its own. They sacrificed to and worshipped other gods (Baals) and burned incense to idols, all of which was forbidden by the Lord. Like any frustrated parent, the Lord chastised Israel for its disobedience. As Hosea recounts the history, Israel was warned of its impending doom. Israel would be destroyed as a nation and taken into captivity as punishment for its wayward ways.

> They shall return to the land of Egypt, and Assyria shall be their king, because they have refused to return to me. The sword shall rage against their cities, consume the bars of their gates, and devour them in their fortresses. My people are bent on turning away from me; so they are appointed to the yoke, and none shall remove it. (Hosea 11:5-7, RSV)

But like any parent who cares for their child, the Lord had second thoughts about punishing his 'child.' Was chastisement and discipline really all that should be done?

> How can I give you up, O Ephraim! How can I hand you over, O Israel! How

can I make you like Admah! How can I treat you like Zeboiim! My heart recoils within me, my compassion grows warm and tender. I will not execute my fierce anger, I will not again destroy Ephraim; for I am God and not man, the Holy One in your midst, and I will not come to destroy. (Hosea 11:8-9, RSV)

Though frustrated in his efforts to lead Israel in the ways of faith, the Lord could not give up on his 'child.' Through Hosea the message was that the Lord would not abandon those he believed to be faithful.

Ephraim has encompassed me with lies, and the house of Israel with deceit; but Judah is still known by God, and is faithful to the Holy One. (Hosea 11:12, RSV)

The larger Northern Kingdom (Ephraim) was destroyed in war, but the Southern Kingdom (Judah) survived. Thus the Lord did not completely abandon the Hebrews, despite the frustrations of his love for them. The faithful remnant of Judah was preserved from the ravages of war.

When a prophet was called to speak to Israel on behalf of the Lord there was more to their calling than just delivering a message. Quite often the prophet had to act out the message in their own lives in a dramatic way. Hosea was commanded by the Lord to choose Gomer as his wife, who was a strong willed and rebellious woman. Several times she left Hosea and ran off with another man, and each time Hosea brought her back, keeping silent during the entire journey home. After several of these episodes Gomer's rebellious heart melted and she accepted the devotion and love Hosea had for her. She eventually gave up her rebellious behavior. The drama of Hosea and Gomer was meant to illustrate God's devotion to Israel, the hope being that Israel would finally see and accept the love the Lord had shown it time and again.

THE LIMITS OF SPIRITUAL LOVE

How does the story of Hosea illustrate self-giving or spiritual love when it is offered with no expectation of reciprocity? It shows that there will be frustrations. Whether it is the Lord pursuing Israel through the Prophets or Hosea going to retrieve Gomer, very often our efforts will meet with rejection and failure. Since most of us are not prophets (or God!) what do we do when our efforts to share spiritual love are thwarted? Our response to rejection will depend on what our purpose is in sharing spiritual love. If we are trying to enhance the spiritual growth of an individual, particularly a romantic partner, it could get painful. The harsh truth is that we cannot force someone to pursue spiritual growth if they do not want to. About the only workable option is to set an example and persevere patiently. This is what Hosea did with Gomer and eventually she responded in a positive way. The Lord did the same with Israel through the Prophets and achieved mixed results. Trying to force spiritual growth on a loved one simply will not work. Sometimes we may decide to give up and walk away, as in the case of Sharon and Ben.

Sharon and Ben had been unhappily married for five years. Ben had a problem with alcohol that was getting worse. Sharon had hoped that the birth of their son James would straighten Ben out, but the added responsibility of a child made his drinking binges worse. Sharon was a devout Christian, and her Bible study group continually prayed for her and Ben. Sharon's Bible study group did not believe in divorce, so they prayed that Ben would renew his faith and deal with his alcoholism. Sharon used to believe that but was not so sure anymore. She had tried to talk to Ben about his problem but he always got mad and left the room. So far Ben had not been violent with Sharon or James when he was drunk, but Sharon was afraid that might change.

One night Ben came home drunk and in a bad mood. He started to throw things around the house. Whether or not it was deliberate, one of the things he threw around was Sharon. It was too much for Sharon to handle, so the next day she and James left, never to return. She filed for divorce from Ben. At first Sharon's Bible study group did not agree with her decision, but they saw her pain and knew she had done all she could. They continued to help her through the difficult months ahead.

How will we know when it is time to give up on our efforts at self-giving spiritual love? I have no easy answers to that question. To give up on self giving spiritual love is a decision that must be made by individuals in particular circumstances. Sharon's dilemma with Ben illustrates the need for maintaining spiritual love relationships beyond romance or marriage. Very seldom are two people at the same level of spiritual maturity in a romance or marriage. Sharon needed to be with people of similar belief and spiritual maturity to meet her individual needs. She might not have had the strength to leave Ben without the support of her Bible study group.

What of self-giving love beyond the individual level, such as political or social action to help the homeless or starving? Like Sharon's situation, patient perseverance and an active support group are essential. Aside from the political power of organized groups, don't forget the need for support. There has to be some group support of spiritual love to keep us going in the face of rejection and set backs. Will self-giving love always meet with rejection and failure? Fortunately, no it will not.

When through its own perseverance self-giving love transforms evil into good, self-giving love becomes redeeming love. The greatest example and the greatest triumph of redeeming love is the age old story of Christ's Crucifixion and Resurrection. In spiritual love, God became human so that humans might become like God. In self-giving love, Christ persevered with his work and message against political and religious opposition, even to the point of death. In redeeming love, a tragic and needless death was transformed into victory through Christ's Resurrection. Similarly, the evil and opposition facing self-giving love can be transformed, resurrected into new opportunities for good, growth, or any of a number of unpredictable new beginnings. We cannot bring about redeeming love on our own, however. Redeeming love is due not just to our efforts, but also to the power of God's presence. When human perseverance and faith combine with God's infinite love, somehow out of this mysterious mix comes the transformation of evil. Perhaps we will never fully understand how such things happen, we will only know that they do. The knowledge that evil can be transformed into good should be enough to keep us going, to keep working at self-giving love. We will not always succeed, but we will not always fail, either. Such is the gamble, and the reward, of self-giving love in this age and in the age to come.

CHAPTER FIVE

COMMUNITY LOVE

"Love is my true identity. Love is my true character. Love is my name."

Laura and Jane had been best friends since they first met in third grade. As they went through junior high and high school they shared everything with each other: new loves, hopes and fears, their dreams for the future. After high school Laura went away to college and Jane stayed back in their home town. They continued to visit each other during vacations when Laura was in town.

One Christmas Laura and Jane got together. Laura sensed that things were different this time, for Jane was usually very talkative and would joke with her. But Jane displayed none of her easy going attitude this time. Instead she was tense and painfully polite. Laura felt Jane came to visit her more because she felt she had to, not because she wanted to. Laura asked her "What is it with you?" Jane answered that she had become a born-again Christian, and she knew Laura had not accepted Jesus Christ as her Lord and Savior. Laura was confused and upset over Jane's attitude towards her. Laura was happy that Jane had found meaning in her Christian faith. Laura herself was agnostic and had no use for organized religion, but she would never let her skepticism get in the way of Jane's new faith or their friendship. What hurt Laura so much was that Jane would let her new found faith ruin their close friendship. Laura thought Christianity was supposed to be about love and compassion, so how could Jane act so cold towards her? Laura never got to ask Jane these questions, because Jane cut off contact with Laura after the Christmas break visit.

Many people in and out of Christianity have encountered this dilemma. Friends or family members who were on good terms for years see relationships torn apart when one of them becomes a "Christian." I have seen this dilemma from both sides. When I was born-again I acted like Jane towards family and friends who were not "believers", at least not according to my definition. And I have seen friends and family whom I openly encouraged to seek Christ turn a harsh heart to me once they "found the Lord." How can a religion supposedly based on love lead to the destruction of genuine friendships? The purpose of this chapter, in part, is to answer that question. We have already explored friendship and spiritual love, so now we must learn the meaning of community or group love as described by community love.

Community love is another kind of love that is introduced by the New Testament. Community love describes the gathering of Christians to sing, worship, preach, and pray in the early church. A key characteristic of community love is that early church communities drew members from different social classes. It was not unusual to have slaves worshipping with merchants or upper class people sitting next to common folk. Spiritual love is an integral part of the practice and understanding of community love, for there was often some concern for the spiritual growth of community members. Putting all of these ideas together, here is the definition of community love.

COMMUNITY LOVE DEFINED

COMMUNITY LOVE: a love characterized by a group based on the belief that all people need and are worthy of spiritual love, with reconciliation and forgiveness as its major goals.

Let us examine this definition phrase by phrase.

Community. One writer suggests that there are three distinct aspects to the church's understanding of community: "support, residence, and service".[30] Community love provides support for the physical and emotional needs of its members when the members assist one another in times of crisis. For example, perhaps one family has lost its major source of income due to layoffs in a bad economy. Members of the community can help the family in need by providing food, money, and emotional support. Many churches provide facilities and support for group programs such as divorce, drug, and alcohol recovery groups.[31]

Community love provides a sense of residence, a place to call home for members of the church community. Regular attendance and participation in church activities widens members' circle of contacts and friends in a city or town. The more people they get to know, the more a city becomes a home instead of just someplace where they live.[32]

Another important aspect of community love is an ethic of caring and action on behalf of those in need, whether in the same town as that of one's church or throughout the world.[33] In the previous chapter we saw that an ethic of caring is also a part of spiritual love because our physical and spiritual needs are inseparable. If spiritual love seeks to enhance the spiritual transformation of others, it cannot neglect the physical needs of people. And if community love believes *all* people need and deserve spiritual love, then this ethic of caring for the physical and spiritual needs of others must extend beyond the immediate religious community. The kind of service the ethic of caring involves can range from donations of money to actual participation in programs, such as the Habitat for Humanity, a program that provides low cost homes for the homeless and poor. Church members often donate materials and labor in the construction of homes through Habitat for Humanity. These and other actions on behalf of the church to help others "promotes an ethic of service that forges chains of caring through various sectors of the community (city or town)."[34]

All People Need and Are Worthy of Spiritual Love. This is the universal note of the Christian faith. The traditional Gospel declares that Christ died for sinful humans, paying for all of their sins with his death upon the Cross. His Resurrection was the promise of eternal life for all who believe in Him. 'Believing' in Christ usually means believing that He is divine, i.e. the Son of God, and that he came on a divine mission to save all humankind from a sentence of death due to their collective and individual sins.

I have trouble with this legal interpretation of the Gospel, for it is here that we develop problems in defining community love. The model of community love a group uses will depend on their understanding of the Crucifixion and Resurrection. If a group buys into the harsh view that *only* those people who believe as *they* do will be saved, chances are they will exhibit Jane's attitude towards nonbelievers. How can this be avoided? By accepting a broader understanding of the Crucifixion and Resurrection.

The idea that the whole Incarnation was brought about merely to pay some cosmic moral or legal debt is only one possible interpretation. The Gospel and Letters of John contain the seeds of a more sophisticated interpretation of the Incarnation, Crucifixion and Resurrection. The interpretation that Christ came in love (spiritual love), was apparently beaten by evil (Crucifixion), and was ultimately victorious over evil (Resurrection) offers more hope.[35] This interpretation still acknowledges the reality of human sin and the need to overcome that sin. Instead of focusing on the negative aspects of sin and the supposed need to pay for it with some sacrifice, the interpretation based on John's writings emphasizes the hope and power of redeeming love over the power of evil. I will discuss the problem of human sin in more detail a little later in this chapter.

The understanding a Christian community has regarding the Crucifixion and Resurrection will determine the key aspects of community love. If a Christian community adopts a siege mentality such as "*We* are the *only* true believers," there is a small problem. First, community love becomes focused on how "we" true believers are different or better than nonbelievers and creates an "us" versus "them" mentality. Second, it adds a distinct note of desperation and judgement in the groups' attempts to convert others. Threats of eternal damnation may figure prominently in their message of salvation. There may even be an angry edge to their pleading "Only those who accept Christ as their Lord and Savior will be saved." But is this the way the message was really meant to be delivered? With anger and desperation?

I remember back to the time when I was not a Christian. I had this angry, desperate version of the Gospel preached in my face many times and it never failed to repulse me. Looking back now from the Christian side of the tracks, I do not feel I rejected the Gospel due to an "evil" heart. If there was any fault to be assigned in my not believing, I lay it squarely with the messengers. If the message is garbled and mangled in its delivery, then the people who fail to receive it are blameless. While being accountable to God for our actions will always be a part of the Gospel, it is the heart or feel of that accountability that is most important. Is God an angry accountant demanding payment for sins at all costs? Or is God a compassionate guide who seeks to create in us the love of Christ for others? It is the latter form of accountability that finally won me over. If God is a compassionate guide then what are the key aspects of community love? Anger and desperation or reconciliation and forgiveness?

Reconciliation. Reconciliation is the belief that all human titles of rank, distinction, status, and so on are secondary to our common need and worthiness of spiritual love. The classic statement of reconciliation is Galatians 3:28:"There is neither Jew nor Greek, there is neither slave nor free, there is neither male nor female; for you are all one in Christ Jesus." Paul is arguing that the salvation offered in Christ is the basis for equality between Jews and Greeks, slaves and freemen, male and female. All humans have a common need for spiritual love, and in the Christian religion the primary source of spiritual love is Christ. Thus the common need of all people for spiritual love, and the one source of spiritual love in Christ provides the basis for reconciliation of all people. This in turn creates a basis for community between all kinds of people. But before reconciliation can take place, there must be forgiveness.

Forgiveness. One of the New Testament Greek terms for 'forgiveness' means literally "to let go, to set free." My interpretation of this is that forgiveness means "to let go from the heart." "Heart" represents that deep core of emotions, attitudes, and values that makes us the distinct individuals we are. "To let go" means to release from concern, obsession, or attention some issue of personal insult, pain, injury, or guilt. It may help to explain forgiveness if I distinguish between two kinds of forgiveness, simple and deep forgiveness.

SIMPLE & DEEP FORGIVENESS

By simple forgiveness I mean the routine forgiveness that we all must practice just to get through the day. Whether it is people we work with, family or friends, people will do things that hurt and upset us. It could be a number of things that occur in daily life, such as arguments or incomplete tasks, that we need to let go and move beyond. If I stopped and fretted over every small insult or injury that came my way each day, I would never get anything accomplished. Simple forgiveness is necessary to maintain working relationships with other people.

Deep forgiveness is far more costly to achieve than simple forgiveness. By deep forgiveness I mean the letting go of deep hurts, angers, fears, grudges, that affect the way we react to other people and how we interpret our experiences. For many of us, the deep hurts date back to our childhood, and it will take a lot of time and effort to overcome them. Fortunately, there is a part of the Christian tradition that makes provision for our need of inner healing.

In the previous chapter on spiritual love, I discussed the contemplative prayer tradition. One of the primary goals of contemplation is to make spiritual love a reality in our relationships with other people. The contemplative tradition is well aware of the fact that many of us, if not most, must first be healed of our own inner pain before we can fully love others. The early stages of contemplative prayer deal mainly with unloading our subconscious of all the anger, fear, guilt, or other burdens we may carry.[36] Coming to terms with the pain of our past not only heals us, but it also slowly turns us outward to other people. In learning of our own needs for healing and forgiveness, we become aware of the need other people have for healing and forgiveness. By forgiving ourselves, we develop compassion for other people in need and learn to forgive them. Compassion, you will recall, is a quality that figures prominently in the definition of spiritual love. Compassion, by way of spiritual love, is also a key component of community love, our life in community with other Christians. Unless we have experienced deep forgiveness in our own lives, we will be limited in our ability to love and forgive others.

With the kind of attitude that Jane showed towards Laura, I wonder if Jane has a well developed sense of compassion? The quality of Jane's compassion will depend on what kind of repentance she has experienced. In traditional Christian theology, repentance means to change the direction of one's life by turning away from the sinful ways of your past. Repentance is the direct result of believing you are forgiven of your sins by Christ, which has usually been associated with the legalistic view of the Crucifixion. This kind of repentance I call the repentance of guilt. The repentance of guilt focuses on all of the terrible things we have done in the past and dwells upon our unworthiness of God's love and forgiveness. The repentance of guilt is certainly one way of receiving the Gospel and becoming Christian. But as one writer put it, this approach dwells too much on the past, for it takes too much energy to keep focusing on the negative side of our sinfulness. I prefer the repentance of joy that comes from the interpretation of the Crucifixion found in the Letters and Gospel of John.

REPENTANCE OF JOY

In the Crucifixion and Resurrection the love of Christ was victorious over the power of sin and death, which should give us a feeling of joy instead of guilt. The repentance of joy looks to the future and what we can become with the help of the Holy Spirit, as expressed in the words of the *Cloud of Unknowing*: "For it is not what you are or have been that God looks at with his merciful eyes, but what you would be." While we do not ignore our sins of the past in the repentance of joy, we leave them behind as we concentrate on what we can become in our spiritual transformation. Compassion is easier to develop in a repentance of joy than repentance of guilt. We learn compassion when we realize how each person, like ourselves, has fears and hopes with which they struggle. Our faith that all people are worthy of and need spiritual love is based on the joy of the Resurrection. Compassion for others is a natural consequence of faith based on the repentance of joy. When faith is based on repentance of guilt, this greatly limits our compassion for others. Compassion is an afterthought in relation to the guilt and desperation with which we perceive other people.

JOY VERSUS GUILT

My first few years as a Christian were spent viewing nonbelievers through the repentance of guilt. I looked down on nonbelievers because they had no idea how "bad" they really were. But a funny thing happened on the way to spiritual transformation. When I learned of the repentance of joy, suddenly I felt more equal to people, both believers and nonbelievers. Surprisingly, I saw that everyone had more or less the same fears and hopes for their lives. What made believers different from nonbelievers was that the latter were simply unaware of the spiritual resources available in spiritual love and community love. The "sudden change" of course had taken place in *me*, not the rest of the world. I can only speculate that Jane had not experienced the repentance of joy. She had not developed that liberating sense of compassion that naturally comes with the repentance of joy. If she had, her attitude towards her life long friend Laura would have been very different.

We learn compassion by seeing how we are *like* other people, which is the basis for the belief that *all* people are worthy of and in need of spiritual love. This understanding of compassion comes from the repentance of joy which in turn rests on the broader understanding of the Crucifixion and Resurrection found in the Gospel and Letters of John. When joy and compassion are the hallmarks of our faith, then reconciliation and forgiveness become the major aspects of community love. The emphasis of community love becomes very different if we cling to the legalistic understanding of the Crucifixion and Resurrection. If sin is something that must be paid for at great cost, we can easily drift into anger and desperation. This effectively destroys feelings of compassion towards other people by those doing the preaching. The legalistic version of the Crucifixion leads people to believe that the first step in preaching the Gospel to others must be to scare them or convince them of their need to pay an unpayable debt. The second step is to intimidate people into believing that this *one* time they are hearing the Gospel is their *only* chance of being "saved."

Part of the desperation and anger that is heard in the preaching of the legalistic Gospel comes from the belief that salvation is a one time possibility. If someone hears a preacher in a church or on the street and they reject the message, the belief is that the listener is doomed forever. But is it that simple? The language of the Gospels is quite clear that belief in Christ is necessary for salvation. What is not so clear is that a person has only one or at best a few chances in this life to believe or not, and then their fate is sealed for eternity. A few New Testament passages imply there are opportunities for accepting Christ even beyond this life. The Now-or-Never emphasis heard in so many versions of Christianity is an oversimplification of the original message. It is precisely at this point where forgiveness and reconciliation vie with anger and desperation as the key ideas of community love. If our faith is comfortable with the mystery and open endedness of God's working in the world, we can see the Now-or-Never version of the Gospel as too simplistic. Hardly anyone can claim to have reached full spiritual development at the time of death, because reconciliation, forgiveness and learning to love are on-going processes. Is it not possible that the journey of faith and love we begin in this life continues in the next? We can never know for sure. A simple "I don't know" should be enough for faith to let go of the Now-or-Never Gospel, and will remove anger and desperation as the key ideas of community love.

So far we have covered the definitions of spiritual love and community love. Much more is involved with these terms than defining them, however. When I say that we all need and are worthy of spiritual love, there are some presuppositions underlying that statement. In particular, there is a certain concept of sin and its remedy that I should make explicit.

THE PROBLEM OF SIN

Sin is not a very popular topic these days, especially among the so-called mainline denominations. Any attempt to locate sin in human nature or human behavior is usually brushed aside as being unsophisticated. Most of us are used to hearing sermons about how good we are, that we are okay and so on. What I am about to say will not exactly be music to many ears, but bear with me. I must first work through the bad news in order to get to the good news.

The Synoptic Gospels are quite clear about human sin. The message, amplified by Paul's letters, is that humans are all sinful. We will all perish after death unless we are saved by some external source that pays for our collective sins. Thus the Crucifixion and Resurrection are explained in legalistic terms, such as Christ was made the ransom or payment for our debt of sinfulness. This interpretation implies that God has a bloodlust to be satisfied regarding humanity's sinfulness. Furthermore, the legalistic interpretation leads to a definition of sin that emphasizes our need to pay an unpayable debt, a repentance of guilt and so on. In contrast, John's interpretation of Christ's Crucifixion and Resurrection focuses on the hope and joy found in spiritual transformation.

Yet this more hopeful approach still recognizes the truth that humans are sinful and in need of change. The definition of sin I am working with comes from the contemplative tradition, which defines sin variously as egocentrism, selfishness, self-centeredness.[37] Self-centeredness refers to the fact that most of us, in most circumstances, will take care of ourselves before anyone else. We are naturally inclined to think, feel, and plan our actions around our own needs above all else. If you think this is natural and good, consider what can be found in the daily papers. Is it normal and good for us to routinely physically and emotionally abuse one another, murder and rob each other? Is it normal and good for us to routinely poison ourselves with various drugs and chemicals, while also poisoning our own planet with industrial waste? Is it normal and good for us to spend large amounts of money to find 50,000 ways to kill our neighbor? All of this points to the idea that there is something fundamentally wrong with us humans. The Synoptic Gospels echo this same idea. Unlike some conservative branches of the Church, however, I do not intend to dwell upon our problems. I am pointing out the severity of the problems so that we have a clear understanding of what we have to work with.

In the movie *Jesus of Nazareth*, John the Baptist put the whole problem succinctly: "Before kingdoms can change, people must change." We may restructure political institutions as much as we wish; we can find some reason to "explain" our inhumanity to each other, be it money, private property, or society; what ever else we do, the problem of human sin remains and needs to be dealt with. The contemplative tradition asserts that through the practice of contemplation, under the guidance and fellowship of other contemplatives, and through the renewing presence of the Holy Spirit, human sin (self-centeredness) can be overcome. It takes a lot of work and it does not happen overnight, but we can grow out of our own self-centered preoccupation and mature in the Spirit and in prayer. There will always be the need for social and institutional reforms, but unless the recurring problem of human sin is dealt with, the institutional changes that come so hard will not last.

CAN PEOPLE LEARN TO BE ALTRUISTIC?

Spiritual transformation sounds like a great deal of work and trouble. Is it really worth all of the hassle? I think a positive answer can be given from an unlikely source: recent sociological studies of altruistic behavior. Morton Hunt summarizes the findings of recent studies on why people behave altruistically, that is, engaging in behavior that benefits others but not necessarily themselves.[38] Hunt does not attempt to answer the philosophical question of whether humans are basically good or evil. He does argue that the findings on altruistic behavior are encouraging.

While humans seem to have an inherent capacity for altruism, individuals display different levels of altruism. Like any other capacity, though, it is subject to a number of influences: environmental influences, such as family upbringing, physical health, and the circumstances of a particular emergency that confronts a potential altruist. Genetics also seems to play a part, with some scientists arguing that there is an inherited helping behavior gene or genes that gives some people a greater potential capacity for altruism than others. The word 'potential' must be emphasized here, for people are not born as fully developed altruists ready to go out and help other people. The major point of the study, and its most encouraging point, is that altruistic behavior is *learned* behavior.[39] People are caring and helpful towards others because they are taught to be that way.

Hunt surveyed several studies on altruistic behavior and found that there were several important ingredients that went into making altruistic people. One important ingredient, which comes as no surprise, is the kind of family life and upbringing a person has as a child. One study focused on people who risked their lives to help save Jews from the Nazis in World War II. The "rescuers," as they were called, were compared to people who did not help save Jews from the Holocaust. Among the findings was the fact that those who had been rescuers had been close to a caring parent as they grew up. The study also found that the caring parent to whom the rescuers were close had also been a "good role model of caring behavior"[40] towards other people. These findings add to many others that confirm the importance of the health and stability of family life in a person's childhood. The study of World War II rescuers also revealed that a rescuer's sense of "extensivity"[41] was a key determinant in their decision to save Jews from the Nazis. The study defined extensivity as "the extent to which caring goes-- how far it reaches out to include outsiders and not just intimates in your in-group, and how strongly you feel that justice is not just for yourself and your own kind but for others beyond your own group."[42] Rescuers tended to have a strong sense of caring and justice that extended beyond their own group. Extensivity is closely related to another key component altruistic behavior, our capacity for empathic and sympathetic responses to others.

Several studies have singled out a person's capacity for empathy or sympathy as perhaps the strongest component of altruistic behavior. Empathy occurs when you personally feel distress and discomfort at seeing someone else who is in pain or suffering. You are reacting with your *own* pain and discomfort at seeing someone else suffer. Sympathy occurs when you put yourself in the place of another person, "projecting" yourself into their point of view, and feel their pain and distress as if it were your own. The question of whether altruism is based primarily on empathy or sympathy is an important one. If empathy is the prime mover, then altruists help others in order to relieve themselves (the altruists) of discomfort. Altruism based on empathy seeks to relieve *our* pain and discomfort at seeing someone else suffer. This would mean altruism occurs to benefit ourselves and not the person suffering, which does not fit our usual definition of altruism. If sympathy is the prime mover, then altruists act out of concern for others, which does meet the traditional expectations of altruistic behavior. Altruism based on sympathy seeks to relieve the pain of the person we see suffering rather than our own pain at seeing someone suffering. In empathy, we stay within our own egocentric world and feel pain at the suffering of others, but it is *our* pain. In sympathy, we reach beyond our egocentric world. Through our imagination, we become the person we see suffering and place ourselves in the pain of the one suffering.

Unfortunately, researchers cannot agree on whether altruism is based on empathy or sympathy. Hunt offers a workable compromise, suggesting that empathy-based sympathy is the prime motivation behind altruism. When we see someone in pain, our first reaction is to feel pain as well, which is <u>our</u> response (empathy) to their suffering. But then we are moved to imagine how it must feel for them (sympathy) to suffer and we put ourselves in their place. We make their pain our own and seek to help them (altruism).

HOW WE LEARN ALTRUISM: COMMUNITY LOVE

These two ideas that researchers have focused upon, extensivity and empathy-based sympathy, have a familiar ring to them. Extensivity is the greatest commandment by another name, "love (spiritual love) thy neighbor as thyself." The empathy-based sympathy that leads to altruistic behavior is the compassion of spiritual love, and the forgiveness and reconciliation of community love, directed towards all humans. Extensivity and empathy-based sympathy are learned behaviors, and thus should be learned in the experience of community love. Certainly there are other places people can learn to be open towards others who are different from them, and learn to have sympathy for the suffering of others. The family and public schools are two such places that come to mind. But the one institution that has had the longest tradition of supposedly teaching extensivity and empathy-based sympathy towards others is the church. In an ideal world, the institutional church and the experience of community love are one and the same. As a minister, I am aware that more often than not, true community love is not a part of the institutional church. Thus there is a double need for community love in the world. Practically, community love can be a powerful source of teaching people the values of extensivity and altruism for other people. Prophetically, there is all the more reason to work for the restoration of community love to the institutional church.

So where does all of this leave Jane and Laura? I have already commented on how Jane may not have experienced the repentance of joy and its related quality of compassion. This would have allowed Jane to feel more of an equal to Laura. But Jane is also making the mistake of confusing friendship with community love. Jane believes that since she is now a Christian she can only have Christian friends. Jane is right in believing she has a need for special community love relationships with people who believe as she does. She is wrong to think her community love relationships must replace *all* of her friendships, for two reasons. First, community love and friendship are two different loves, so the specific goals of each love are distinct. Friendship meets the most basic need we all have for human companionship. Community love is more focused, for it seeks to meet our need for spiritual transformation and community. Secondly, it goes against the spirit of community love to reject all of one's nonbelieving friends. If we have developed compassion from a repentance of joy, and reconciliation and forgiveness are our goals, how can we justify rejecting our nonchristian friends? While we welcome our relationships found in spiritual love and community love, we do not say goodbye to our various friends. To be a complete human being we need them all, for such is the variety and the beauty of the different loves.

CHAPTER SIX

JEALOUSY

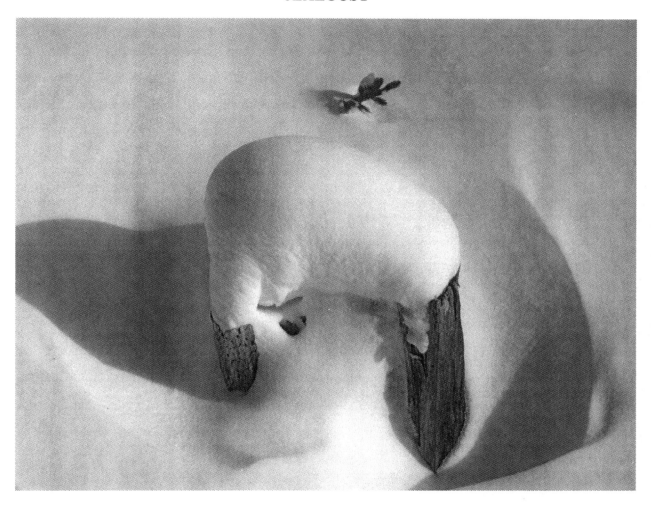

"The intensity of jealousy is caused by viewing intimacy as a zero-sum game."

Kara and John were the model professional couple.

Both were successful ministers in different denominations, and each had their own church. Their busy schedules kept them apart, but they spent what time they could with each other and their kids. Several years into their marriage, things began to change.

Kara felt she needed some time off from their relationship. She moved out of the family house and into her own apartment. John was furious, but felt he had no choice but to comply. Kara and John continued to see a marriage counselor during the separation. As the weeks turned into months, John's anger at Kara grew. He kept asking when was she coming home? She kept saying she did not know.

Kara finally decided to file for divorce from John. When John heard of Kara's decision, something seemed to snap inside of him. Several of his friends heard him comment "If she won't have me, she won't have anyone!"

The end came one quiet Spring evening. It was Sunday and Kara was meeting with the high school students of her church. After the meeting, Kara was talking with several of her students on the front lawn of the church. As she was talking, she noticed John get out of his car that was parked in front of the church. As he approached, she could tell by the look on his face he was very upset. As he came closer, Kara noticed John had something in his hand. It was a gun. With little time to do anything, Kara screamed. John shot her down in front of her students. He then walked back to his car, got in, and shot himself.

How could a seemingly strong relationship end in such a deadly way? What caused John to feel so desperate that he had to kill both himself and Kara? Part of the answer is the no-so-neat part of love: jealousy.

If there is one emotion that makes me want to be like Mr. Spock from Star Trek, it is jealousy. Mr. Spock relied on pure logic and had no need of emotions. Unfortunately, we humans cannot escape our emotions, including jealousy. Everyone feels it to some extent, especially regarding the ones we love. While jealousy seems to be a part of love, it can become destructive of the very love it seeks to protect. In this chapter we will take a closer look at jealousy and try to understand why it can become so destructive.

JEALOUSY DEFINED

Jealousy can include a wide range of experiences. We can be jealous of someone else's clothing, money, looks, friends, family members, to give only a few examples. I will focus upon the jealousy involved with love relationships. To begin, here is my definition of jealousy:

JEALOUSY: a fear of losing the affections and attention of a loved one to a real or imagined rival.[43]

Let us take a closer look at this definition.

Fear of Losing. Putting it in the simplest terms, jealousy is basically a fear of loss. The circumstances under which we can feel jealousy will vary. We might be children feeling jealous towards siblings, or adults feeling jealous towards our lover or a close friend. What ever the circumstances, our jealousy is basically a fear of loss, specifically the fear of losing the special relationship we have with someone for whom we care very much.

The Affection or Attention of a Loved One. Jealousy usually arises in the context of relationships to people we love. All love relationships are not created equal. As mentioned in the chapter on friendship, the key difference between friends, on the one hand, and family and romantic partners, on the other hand, is the level of availability we find in the various relationships. When we feel jealousy, we fear the loss of the exclusivity[44] of affection and attention of a best friend, romantic partner, or family member. The deeper and more exclusive we feel our relationship is, the greater the intensity of the jealousy we will feel. What we fear is the loss of our relationship.

To a Real or Imagined Rival. For us to feel jealousy, there must be a rival that we perceive as a threat to our love relationship. The rival may be very real, such as a new and possible love interest who might divert one's romantic partner. Or the rival may not be a person but a thing, such as a job or illness. Jealousy can also arise when we imagine there is a rival when in fact there is none. Jealousy becomes most destructive when we create rivals out of our own fearful imaginations. We end up wasting time and energy fretting over a threat that does not even exist. John was furious at the prospect of losing Kara's affections to someone else. He was so dependent on Kara, he could not survive (so he thought) without her. This is jealousy at its worst extreme. Is this the same or different from another no-so-neat feeling, envy?

JEALOUSY & ENVY

Curt and Bill were the best of friends. When they finished high school, Bill decided to go into the family owned used car business. Curt wanted to be a lawyer, so he left town to pursue his education. Ten years after their high school graduation Curt came back to his hometown to start his own law business.

Curt and Bill had kept in touch over the years. Bill secretly became more and more angry at Curt's apparent success as compared to his own lack of it. Curt had a beautiful wife and two wonderful kids. Curt's new law firm in their hometown was getting off to a great start. Bill had not done quite as well by comparison. He took over the car dealership when his father died a few years before. The business had been losing money the last few years due to the extended recession and competition from foreign cars. Bill's financial situation was worsened by the fact that he had to pay alimony to support his ex-wife and son. Bill thought to himself one day, "Curt is my best friend, but I sure am jealous of him."

What Bill was feeling towards Curt was not jealousy, but a close cousin, envy. Envy is often confused with jealousy. Envy is usually defined as a strong desire to acquire a quality or thing someone else has, but that is not in our possession.[45] Envy is usually focused upon the quality or thing one does not possess, and thus is directed towards the person we perceive as a rival.[46] For example, we might envy someone else's musical talent, good looks, or education. Our envy, or desire to have what our rival has, focuses upon the talent, looks, or education that we do not have but wish we had. Envy arises out of comparing ourselves to others we think are better off than we are.[47] In contrast, jealousy is over a person we love and our relationship with them. Our jealousy is directed towards the person we care about instead of the person we consider to be our rival. What John felt towards Kara was jealousy. He deeply feared the loss of her affections to someone else. In contrast, what Bill was feeling towards Curt was envy. Bill was not afraid of losing the affections of a significant other to Curt. Instead, Bill desired for himself the same success, financial and personal, that Curt had. Bill wanted what Curt had but that he did not. John feared losing what he had, Kara's affections, to someone who did not yet possess those affections. This is the major difference between jealousy and envy.

Envy can be good or bad. As one writer put it, there is "malicious envy" and "admiring envy."[48] "In the case of malicious envy, one wants to lower the other (to one's own level or below); in the case of admiring envy, one wishes to raise oneself (to become like the other)."[49] Malicious envy bears animosity, even hatred towards the rival. Malicious envy thus serves no useful purpose in our relationships with other people. Admiring envy is constructive. It can inspire us to improve ourselves, challenging us to grow by emulating the one we admire. Whether Bill felt good or bad envy towards Curt depends on what Bill did with those feelings. If Bill felt hostility and bitterness towards Curt, Bill had succumbed to bad envy. If Bill decided to quit the family business and pursue something more lucrative, then Bill experienced good or admiring envy.

The distinction between jealousy and envy is important in order to know what emotion we are experiencing. We will feel envy equally towards people we know well and people who are total strangers. We will feel jealousy towards people we love much and know well, and it is this which I want to deal with in the larger context of the different loves.

THE EXPERIENCE OF JEALOUSY

So far we have a definition of jealousy, but what about the experience of jealousy? What is the content of the emotion of jealousy? Jealousy usually begins as a series of questions that occur to us. We see our loved one interacting with and drawing close to our suspected rival, and a flood of questions fills our mind. "What is missing in our relationship?" "What is my rival providing that I am not?" "Are there things my loved one can say to my rival that my loved one cannot say to me?" "Do we really share everything?" and so on.[50] When we start asking ourselves these questions in conjunction with our fear of losing our love relationship, we are experiencing jealousy. John most likely began experiencing jealousy by being bombarded with intense questions and doubts. "Am I not good enough for Kara? Is there something I haven't done? Is there someone else?" Is it good or bad to feel this fear of loss and to be bothered by these questions?

Jealousy, like envy, has a good and bad side to it. Jealousy is good in at least two ways. First, jealousy can be "a sign of love. It reflects a positive evaluation of, or attachment or commitment to the person one is jealous over or about."[51] When we feel jealous about someone, we may realize for the first time that we love them. Second, jealousy shows us that there are "material conditions"[52] of love, that there are limits to love at the individual level. For an individual love relationship to flourish, there are limits that must be respected and maintained. Two such limits are time and attention.[53] For intimacy to grow, two people must spend time together and build a personal history of shared experiences with each other. The kind of focused attention that intimacy requires takes energy and concentration. "One can only devote so much 'loving care' at any given moment."[54] If we are constantly distracted by job, activities, or problems, the distraction will take its toll on intimacy and interfere with our love relationship. Thus jealousy can be a warning sign that we may be bumping up against the material limits of love that allow our intimacy to flourish. Certainly this was part of John's experience of jealousy. He knew that the longer Kara and he were separated the more their relationship would suffer. Time apart meant time not devoted to intimacy. It was hard enough to find time for each other when they were living together. Being separated only made it harder on their relationship.

Jealousy does have its good side in showing us that we really do care for someone, and that love has material limits that must be respected if it is to flourish. Unfortunately, our experience of jealousy is not always so positive. It often becomes so intense that it destroys the very relationship it would supposedly preserve. This is what happened with John in his jealousy towards Kara. What may have started as understandable jealousy eventually became destructive and fatal. When do we cross the line from good jealousy to bad jealousy? When our jealousy becomes obsessive, when significant portions of our waking time and energy are devoted to thinking and ruminating about our jealousy. We "generate a set of obsessive scenario-constructing thoughts. These thoughts generally involve the construction of vivid stories, with the jealous person as a voyeur of an endless series of vignettes that cause (them) pain."[55] John probably became immobilized by his constant worrying, picturing in his mind what Kara might be doing with whom. Why does jealousy become so obsessive, and can this obsessiveness be overcome? Like any emotion, jealousy is complex, which means there are no simple answers in dealing with the bad side of jealousy. However, I do believe we can achieve a general understanding of why jealousy goes bad and what might be some possible solutions to the problem.

WHY JEALOUSY IS SO CONSUMING

Part of the consuming nature of jealousy is that when we experience the nagging questions of jealousy, we assume the answers to the questions are all negative.[56] Even though we will wonder "What is missing? What am I doing wrong?" the answers may be that nothing is missing, nothing is wrong. As mentioned in the chapter on friendship, we need to maintain our friendships beyond our romantic, family, and marriage relationships. There are needs that only friends can fulfill, such as detached and objective feedback, that our more involved love relationships cannot fulfill. And as paradoxical as it may seem, the friendships we maintain will serve to strengthen our more involved love relationships. No one person can fully meet the needs of another, most especially in the more intense loves of romance, family, and marriage. Recognizing our common need of both friends and romantic partners will hopefully defuse some of the panic we feel when we experience jealousy. Part of the mistake John made was to rely too heavily on his relationship with Kara to fulfill his needs. Of course, it is normal to rely more on a romantic partner than a friend for many of our needs. Yet if we do not maintain a few active friendships, our reliance upon our romantic partner can become too much. While John would understandably feel great pain at his separation from Kara, it was not inevitable that his pain would become fatal. If John had been more emotionally invested in active friendships perhaps the outcome would have been different. This may not have saved their marriage, but Kara and John might still be alive today and getting on with their lives.

A related mistake we often make in our frenzy of questions is that we "confuse something with everything."[57] Simply because there is "something" between our loved one and a possible rival does not mean it is the end of everything between us and our loved one. Referring again to the chapter on friendship, intimacy is part of *all* of the loves. Just because we are intimate with other close friends does not mean that we automatically diminish the unique intimacy we share with our romantic, family, or marriage partner. As important as these suggestions may be in helping to keep our perspective about jealousy, they still do not alleviate the intensity of jealousy.

Where does the consuming intensity of jealousy come from? Why do we so often fall into obsessive ruminating about our loved one and a possible rival? Part of the intensity of jealousy comes from our perception, right or wrong, that our very identity, the "I-ness" of me, is under attack. To simply imagine that we may lose an important love relationship leaves us feeling that we are losing an integral part of our self.[58] The panicked sense of losing our identity is due, in turn, to at least two other things: our tendency to identify our self with valued things and valued people, and the belief that relationships are a zero-sum game.

It is natural to think of our self identity as being made up of the "things" we feel are important to us. The way we view ourselves is greatly influenced, even dependent upon, the things and people we value most. Whether it is our job, spouse and children, friends, material possessions, level of personal wealth, all of these things are a part of our self image. In suffering the loss of any or all of the examples just mentioned, we feel that we are losing a part of who we are. Rightly or wrongly, when our self image depends on so many externals we become enmeshed in the zero-sum game approach to life.

We are engaged in zero-sum game thinking when we think "if I am to gain someone else must lose." Or, as it applies to jealousy, "if my loved one becomes close to someone else, it will be at my expense." This is more of an emotional, half conscious belief than it is a rational thought. We feel, we fear, that there is only a limited supply of wealth, success, or love to go around. If someone else succeeds in their job, wealth, or love, it can only be at our expense. If our self image is heavily dependent upon externals, and we buy into a zero-sum game approach to love, it is no wonder that jealousy is so intense. We experience jealousy as a panicked sense of an all encompassing attack upon our very identity as a person. We not only fear the loss of our love relationship, we also fear the destruction of ourselves as a result of the potential loss of love. This apparently is the trap into which John fell in his jealousy towards Kara. His own personal identity depended too much upon his relationship with Kara. John must have felt on the verge of losing himself during the entire separation. But he poured fuel on the flames of his fear by obsessing over his jealousy. Buying into the zero-sum approach to intimacy, John must have convinced himself there was, or will be, someone else to replace him. When Kara decided upon divorce, John felt his own individual existence also came to an end. He then gave in to the convoluted logic that only makes sense to a desperate, fear filled mind: If she leaves, I die; If I die, so must she.

How can we overcome this panicked sense of attack on our self identity in the experience of jealousy? As I have already pointed out, jealousy is a complex emotion, and there are no simple answers in alleviating jealousy. I believe, however, that if we can somehow become less dependent upon externals in defining our self image, and let go of the zero-sum game approach to life and love, the intensity of our jealousy will be reduced. It is here that the contemplative prayer tradition can be very helpful.

ZERO-SUM THINKING AND THE FALSE SELF

A major goal of contemplative prayer is to free us from our "false" self and become our "true" self, a person able to love and give more freely. What constitutes the false self? The false self is constituted by at least three things: the fantasy ideal self, the egocentric need to control, and family and cultural expectations.

The fantasy ideal self is something we all grow up with from childhood. It usually starts with a favorite hero we admire and wish to emulate, such as an athlete, artist, movie star, or wealthy person. We want to be like our hero, and we fantasize about how we want to be, incorporating into our fantasy ideal self achievements and/or traits of our hero. This fantasy ideal self has great power over our self-image and self-esteem. The fantasy ideal self of childhood carries over into adulthood and continues to effect the way we view ourselves. We evaluate ourselves by the level to which we make our heroes' traits and achievements our own. We thus equate the "real me" to externals. Am I as wealthy, famous, or successful as my fantasy ideal self tells me I should be? If others are successful or even do better than we do, we see their success as our loss. Zero-sum game thinking slips in, and we fear the success of others will be at our expense.

When I was a child, I decided I wanted to become a brilliant research scientist in physics. I read everything I could find about Albert Einstein, Michael Faraday and other famous physicists. I tried to imitate in my own life some of the unusual qualities I saw in their lives. Quite a few of the famous physicists were very shy and reclusive by nature. This suited me fine since I was painfully shy as a child. The famous physicists I read about also spent much of their time working on physics problems and experimenting in their labs. As I got into chemistry, math and physics in high school and college, I too spent much of my time in the lab and working on physics problems. Unfortunately, this was not due to my genius as a physicist. The simple truth was that it took me forever to figure out what the heck was going on! This fantasy ideal self I had of being a research physicist had enormous power over me well into college. After several years of C grades (and a few D's) in math and physics, I became quite bitter. I grew more and more angry and envious of other physics students who did better than me. Eventually I realized I was becoming someone I did not like. The anger was bad enough. It was the growing sense of dread that other students' success was at my expense that finally made me re-examine my fantasy ideal self. In the end I had to let go of my childhood dream of becoming a physicist. My talents and destiny lay in another direction.

When we fail to live up to out fantasy ideal self, we fall prey to zero-sum thinking. "Someone else's success comes at my expense." What lies behind this zero-sum thinking? An exaggerated notion of how much control we have over our lives and destiny. In other words, our egocentric need to control is in back of zero-sum thinking.

The egocentric need to control is a direct result of the natural self-centeredness into which we are all born. Our general attitude towards life is that "the self [the 'real me'] exists only in my egocentric desires, is the fundamental reality of life to which everything else in the universe is ordered."[59] When we equate the "real me" with our natural egocentric desire to control, it is natural to feel that *anything* that gets in the way of satisfying our desires diminishes the "real me." Thus the soil is cultivated for the tendency to equate the "real me" with externals that satisfy my desires: money, status, job, relationships, awards, and so on. Take any of these externals away and you dissect the "real me." The zero-sum way of thinking comes into play as well. We feel that we must compete with everyone else who seeks to meet their desires. If they win, if they succeed, it can only be at my expense. We feel this is a finite world with only so much love, wealth, and success to go around.

Our natural desire to control creates a lot of needless grief. We begin our journey in life thinking we have far greater control that we really do. The reality of things soon catches up with us. No matter how badly I *wished* to become a straight 'A' physics major it was not going to happen. I did not have the ability in physics I thought I did. As mentioned before, we humans cannot escape our emotions like Mr. Spock. When our exaggerated sense of control *and* our exaggerated expectations from our fantasy ideal self collide with reality, we find ourselves in trouble. If our entire self image is wrapped up in our fantasy ideal self, we measure ourselves by externals or the lack thereof: money(almost enough or too little), prestige(almost enough or too little), significant others(almost enough or too little) and so on.

Since almost no one lives up to their ideals, what are we to do? Reassert, however absurdly, our belief we can control our destiny? The fear that someone else's success comes at my expense comes from a desperate desire to believe we *do* control our destiny. The more we fail to live up to our fantasy ideal self, the more we assert our belief in our ability to control. This spiral can go down and down until, at its extreme, we destroy ourselves as well as others. John fell into this deadly spiral. His identity was measured by his marriage to Kara. The more his marriage unraveled, the more desperate he became to reassert his exaggerated sense of control. When the situation slipped out of his control he made one last desperate effort to control: he destroyed.

How can we escape this vicious spiral of not succeeding to control? Before we can answer that question we have to cover one more factor that contributes to this spiral.

Besides the fantasy ideal self and our egocentric need to control, the false self is also constituted by family and cultural expectations. Each one of us has been raised in a particular family and culture, with specific expectations placed upon us from an early age. As an example of family expectations, some people might be raised with the belief that they would carry on the family business. Perhaps your parents wanted you to enter a 'respectable' profession, such as law, medicine, or business, instead of the theater or arts. Bill was under a lot of pressure to enter the family auto business. When his father died, he must have felt even more pressure to take over as manager of the business. His envy of Curt was due, in part, to the career freedom Curt had but he did not.

Cultural expectations are harder to pinpoint but their influence upon us is just as real. For example, men might be encouraged to enter the more intellectual professions such as science and engineering, while women are encouraged to enter 'nurturing' professions, such as teaching and nursing. Family and cultural expectations heavily influence our self-image, particularly our fantasy ideal self. We again identify ourselves by externals. If we are not successful in an acceptable profession, we may feel as though the "real me" is a total failure. Zero-sum thinking kicks in when we feel envy towards those who have the opportunities or success we lack. The success of others must be at the expense of the "real me." When we cling tenaciously to our fantasy ideal self, and continue unhindered to identify the "real me" with the egocentric control of our life, we are ripe for the experience of intense obsessive jealousy.

> As long as you have to defend the imaginary self that you think is important, you lose peace of heart. As soon as you compare that shadow with the shadows of other people, you lose all joy, because you have begun to trade in unrealities, and there is no joy in things that do not exist.[60]

The false self, the "real me" that we fear is being attacked in our experience of jealousy, is based upon a complicated illusion. The illusion is built upon our youthful fantasies, our natural self-centeredness, and cultural and family expectations. How do we unravel the twisted tapestry of the false self and rediscover our true self? In a way that, at first glance, sounds paradoxical. We must first learn how we are like other people before we can learn how we are different.

JEALOUSY DECREASES AS COMPASSION INCREASES

"We should recognize in every other human being the same nature, the same needs, the same destiny as in ourselves."[61] In the early stages of contemplative prayer, the key virtue that we are taught is compassion. We see honestly, perhaps for the first time in our lives, how we are a mixture of healthy and unhealthy motives, needs, hopes and fears. As the Spirit patiently shows

69

us our particular matrix of motives, needs, hopes and fears, something unusual happens. We begin to see that other people are also a mixture of healthy and unhealthy motives, needs, hopes, and fears. These revelations that we are all in the same situation produces a great sense of freedom within ourselves and in our attitude toward others. Why do we need to compete and fight others when we are each struggling with our own matrices of healthy and unhealthy motives, needs, hopes, and fears? When we see how we are all struggling with a similar burden, compassion is born. We begin to experience spiritual love in our first steps towards spiritual growth. As we unravel the twisted tapestry of our own false self, we see that others are trying to and need to do the same in their own lives as well. In our compassion, we see the universal need for spiritual growth, and the corresponding need to provide the conditions that promote spiritual growth in others. Thus our first inkling of compassion leads to an awareness of the need for spiritual love. As we learn of our own need for spiritual growth we also learn that we cannot accomplish such growth on our own. We need the company and support of other people who are also seeking to grow spiritually. Thus our first experience of spiritual love leads to a desire for community love.

I cannot help but wonder how different things would have been if John had been able to express his fears to Kara. Certainly Kara must have had fears of her own that lead her to move out. The natural response of our egocentric need to control is to cling to our false self when we feel threatened. At its extreme, the false self may flee, as Kara was doing. Or the false self may seek to destroy, as John did. If we have developed our sense of compassion, we have one more option in our response to the fears jealousy may bring up within us. Instead of running or destroying, we can stay with the relationship. Why stay with it? Because we have let go of the false self enough to see how our fears and needs are the same as those of the one we love. And we can see that two people together have greater potential of facing and conquering these fears and needs than they do alone. If John and Kara had been able to share their fears and needs, and view with compassion their mutual struggle, who knows what the outcome would have been. In a roundabout way the struggle with jealousy and the false self brings us to the need for spiritual love and community love. These two loves cannot remove the struggles and fears we all must face in our love relationships. But spiritual love and community love can give us the strength to work through these fears and struggles rather than giving into them.

Once we begin to see how we are like other people, we can learn how we are different. Once the egocentric desire to control begins to ease, we can sort through the expectations of our fantasy ideal self, our family and our culture. We choose which motivations and hopes to maintain, we see what fears and needs are real and which ones are illusions. We can accept the abilities and talents we have rather than wishing for and daydreaming about ones we do not have. The guiding light in our discovery of our true self is not simply getting what we want out of life or only self-actualization, though these are by-products of the discovery of our true self. As the Spirit leads us on the path from the false self to the true self, the guiding principle is love. "Love is my true identity. Selflessness is my true self. Love is my true character. Love is my name."[62]

The primary love that is being reproduced within us is spiritual love in relation to community love. As we grow away from the false self to the true self however, we also develop a greater capacity for the other loves. As we free ourselves from the twisted tapestry of the false self we have more emotional energy available. We are no longer caught in the endless cycle of having to defend our false self. As we become more aware of our true self, there is less of a tendency to identify the "real me" with things and people that we value. Consequently, we are less inclined to view relationships in terms of a zero-sum game. When we no longer identify the self with the things we value, our panic and fear of personal annihilation in the face of jealousy should diminish. The false self, which is the basis of our fear of personal annihilation, is being dismantled. As a result, there is less of a need to invest our emotions in defending the false self through intense obsessional jealousy.

If John had not been so consumed in protecting his false self, the energy he put into his anger could have been channeled differently. Since he was so emotionally invested in believing the "real me" was his fragile, egocentric false self, he *felt* that the only option was to destroy. But if he had made some effort to dismantle the false self, he would have felt there were other options besides obsessional jealousy and its frenzy of running away or destroying. He would not have felt the need to identify so heavily with Kara and their relationship. Perhaps the hole he felt in his identity created by the separation could have been filled another way. What he viewed only as a loss to him, with Kara moving out (zero-sum thinking), could have become a new opportunity. If the two of them could have seen more clearly their common needs and fears, the separation could have been a chance to restructure their relationship.

CAN JEALOUSY BE ERADICATED?

Does all of this spiritual growth eradicate jealousy completely? No, unfortunately it does not. If you ever love someone, be they lover, friend, or family, you will feel some jealousy. In the first chapter I mentioned that we bring our best and worst qualities to all of our love relationships, and that we have mixed motives in our loves. Jealousy, unfortunately, is one of those not-so-neat items that we bring with us to our love relationships. But if we make the effort to grow spiritually in contemplative prayer, one of the side benefits can be to diminish the burning fire, the frenzied panic of obsessional jealousy. Often there are other factors that contribute to obsessional jealousy that require the help of a therapist. Yet, I do believe that growth towards spiritual maturity and the unraveling of the false self can help to bring intense obsessional jealousy under control.

Another side benefit of spiritual growth is that as the need for egocentric control declines, there should be a greater ability to control our desires. Spiritual growth will not and should not do away with the desires for sex, food, and emotional affirmation. Instead, the unraveling of the twisted tapestry of the false self may help to dismantle inordinate desires that we may have struggled with in the past. Sometimes we feel compulsive or insatiable desires for food, sex, or emotional support (among other things) that can become addictions. The compulsive or addictive desire for something may be an unconscious defense or compensation on our part to cover up some deep hurt or fear that is part of the false self. Part of the frenzy John felt came from his addiction or compulsive desire to cling to his relationship with Kara. John was using his relationship with Kara to cover up or fill in some unmet emotional needs of his own. Rather than face his own unmet needs, his relationship with Kara became a safe but unfulfilling substitute. I do not want to suggest that spiritual growth is a cure all for complex problems. But often in following the path of contemplation, part of the healing process involves coming to terms with and releasing behavior patterns that contribute to compulsive or addictive desires. Such inner healing can only improve our ability to enter into male/female friendships. Indeed, C.S. Lewis himself believed that the spiritual maturity that comes with spiritual love liberates all of the other loves to be shared in a deeper, more fulfilling way.[63] This is simply a more elegant way of saying that our progress from the false self to the true self helps to free us from the need for egocentric control in all of our love relationships.

CHAPTER SEVEN

MARITAL AND FAMILY LOVE

"I believe in you. I believe in who you are and in who you can become."

For many people, marital and family love are experienced together. Whether as children of their parents or parents of their children, the two loves seem inseparable. As closely linked as they are, family and marital love are distinct from one another. I must do more than simply give definitions to these two loves, however. With divorce rates still high, and never ending horror stories being told of various family dysfunctions, marital and family love are both facing some serious difficulties. In the discussion on marital love, I will offer some thoughts on how *not* to attain marital love as well as how to attain and maintain marital love. I will also offer some ideas on the nature and practice of family love and how I hope that it can be successfully reached by more people. I will start by giving my definition of marital love.

MARITAL LOVE DEFINED

MARRIAGE: a love that is primarily characterized by a companionship devoted to sustaining the physical, emotional, and spiritual needs of both partners over a lifetime.

If I could express in one word what I believe to be the heart of a marriage relationship, it is the word companionship. Companionship connotes a relationship between equals, where each shares with the other. Companionship means that we have found someone to be with, to do things with, to accompany us through life. The basis for this companionship is our natural need to be with someone in order to meet our emotional, physical and spiritual needs over time. We all have the need to be affirmed, to *feel* that we are important and acceptable as human beings. We find this affirmation in others and with others for whom we care. We learn of our good and bad qualities in the give and take of love shared with other people. In a similar way, we depend upon others to help meet our physical needs such as food, clothing, shelter, touching and being touched. Our spiritual needs are also met by a network of relationships in community. Prayer, worship, faith, are all things that we learn from and practice with others of similar beliefs.

Companionship and a natural and basic need for other people to help us maintain our emotional, physical, and spiritual well being; these are the bases for my definition of marriage. There is nothing unusual about the desire for companionship and the need for people in our lives, so what is it that makes marital love unusual as compared to the other loves? It is the same quality that distinguishes friends from best friends, family from friends, and best friends from lovers: availability. It is the depth of our commitment to the one whom we love that sets marital love apart from all other loves. Different religions offer varying theological justifications for marriage, but in the end it may come down to sheer practicality. As I discussed in the chapter on jealousy, there are material conditions of love. Two of those material conditions are limits to the time and energy we can expend on love relationships. Because of our finite nature, we can only focus our need for and special efforts toward intimacy on one person. This is not to take away from the importance of the choice we make in a lifetime partner, nor does it diminish the momentous event when we find our life long companion. I emphasize the practicality of marital love because I think it is *natural* for the vast majority of us humans to desire and seek a lifetime companion.

In our culture at least, marital love is seen as an outgrowth of romantic love. So when does romantic love become marital love? Quite simply, when we *decide* that the romantic love we share is a love that we want to sustain indefinitely. And how do we know when we have a romantic love that we should want to make a marital love? I refer you to the first chapter where I suggested three criteria for determining whether or not you are in love: Do you love them because you need them or do you need them because you love them?; it is not just how much you love someone, but who you are when you are with them; and the essence of love is a sense of sanctuary. While these are characteristic of all the loves, I believe the three criteria should be met before a romantic love can become a marital love. If these criteria are not met, I would question the reasons for and the sincerity of the commitment involved in your romantic love that would become marital love.

This covers my definition of marital love. As we shall see, the easy part is saying what constitutes marital love. The hard part comes in answering the questions "How do you achieve marital love, and once there, how do you maintain it?" This question is more than a matter of practical philosophy and definitions. Considering the fact that the divorce rate is hovering around 50%, the question of how to love and maintain marital love has a certain urgency. To begin, I will first explain how not to attain marital love before I argue how it is attained.

HOW TO ACHIEVE LASTING LOVE?

Within the popular literature on love and relationships I have noticed a recurring pattern or theme on how one achieves a lasting (usually meant marital) love relationship. I have run across several variations of this pattern in books, seminars, and tapes on the subject of love relationships. For lack of a better name, I will call this pattern the popular model for attaining love. I cannot attribute this pattern to any one author, so this summary is my own rendition of the pattern or theme. The pattern for achieving lasting love goes something like this:

Before you can achieve a lasting and fulfilling love relationship, you must first actualize yourself. This is done by dealing with your dysfunctional background. 95% of all families are dysfunctional, so you are more than likely in need of working through your particular dysfunction. Group therapy, individual therapy or both are needed to overcome your particular dysfunction. If you do not work through your dysfunction, you will continue to pick unhealthy and unfulfilling partners. Once you have worked through your dysfunction and actualized yourself, you will then be able to choose a partner for a healthy and fulfilling relationship.

I have several objections to this argument, not the least of which is that it is so depressing a scenario. The figure of 95% of all families being dysfunctional is used quite freely, but I have doubts as to its reliability. I have yet to see a clear statement of what constitutes 'dysfunction.' The term could cover anything from sexual, physical, verbal and/or substance abuse to mild insecurities. At least one authority offers a more negotiable range of 80-95% of families being dysfunctional.[64] Assuming for the sake of argument that the 95% figure is accurate, where does that leave us? How do we work through our dysfunctional background? Why, therapy, of course. Individual therapy, group therapy, take your pick. But there is yet another problem: many people cannot afford therapy. When I have asked some therapists about the financial burden this places upon some people, the response is often "If it is important to you, you will find the money." Unfortunately, many people do not have the money, period. But assuming for the sake of argument that you do have the money and you do go through therapy, how long does it take to work through our dysfunction and achieve psychological health? Months? Years? How do we know when we are cured? Most of the psychological models I am familiar with put 'maturity' occurring no earlier than the late thirties or early forties at best. But assuming that you successfully completed therapy, where does that leave you? Even if you have worked through your dysfunction and are now capable of a fulfilling love relationship, you have to find someone else who has *also* gone through therapy and worked through their dysfunction. I do not even want to attempt to figure the dismal odds that leaves you with.

The consequences of the popular model of attaining love are profound. According to the model, the vast majority of our population first needs therapy before they can attain a lasting love relationship. Unfortunately, a large segment of the population has no hope of attaining lasting love relationships because they fall below the socio-economic level that can afford therapy. Assuming you are among the fortunate minority who can afford therapy and have worked through your dysfunction, you face dismal odds of finding a compatible person who has also successfully negotiated the gauntlet of therapy and dysfunction. This puts the hope of attaining lasting love relationships beyond the reach of too many people, and this is why I reject the popular model for achieving lasting love.

While my objections are many, I must be sure to say that there is indeed a need for many people to have access to therapy before they can have any hope of attaining lasting love relationships. The statistics as to how many people come from backgrounds of physical, sexual, verbal and/or substance abuse are staggering. There clearly is a need and place for therapy in helping people overcome dysfunctional backgrounds. I am not arguing that there is no need for therapy in learning to overcome dysfunction in order to attain lasting love relationships. What I am arguing is that the popular model of attaining love offered by many therapists is incomplete. We need to distinguish between mythical ideals and the facts of our day to day existence.

THE MYTH OF THE INDIVIDUAL

In the popular model of attaining love there often occurs a myth of the individual that is held as the goal of treatment. By myth, I do not mean a fictional account that is not true regarding some person or event. When I use the term myth I mean an ideal we strive for, realizing that we will never fully attain the ideal all of the time. The myth of the individual holds that we cannot really love others until we first learn to love ourselves.[65] Until we first self-actualize ourselves in therapy, deal with our insecurities, neuroses, addictions, and other assorted dysfunctions, we will not find lasting love. We are doomed to repeat our self-defeating behaviors in unfulfilling relationships until we self-actualize or heal our dysfunctions. The problem with the myth of the individual is that we run into a paradox. The recurring personal issues that supposedly prevent a dysfunctional person from finding lasting love relationships usually come up *in relationships* with other people. The myth of the individual holds that we first self actualize, *then* go and find a lasting love relationship. The facts of our daily existence are such that we *need* loving relationships--friends, family, romantic partner--whether or not we are self-actualized. In theory, we first deal with personal issues of dysfunction, then go back into love relationships. In practice, we will encounter personal issues of dysfunction in relationships that we need and are on-going. How do we get around this paradox? By realizing that the major point of the myth of the individual is more attainable than the popular would lead us to believe: there is a minimal level of emotional health that is necessary before one can engage in meaningful love relationships of any kind. What is that minimal level of emotional health? Let me answer that question by way of practical illustration.

When I was in seminary, all of the ministry students were required to take some counseling courses. The purpose of the counseling courses was to teach us future ministers listening skills to assist any parishioners who came to us with their problems. We were also admonished to use our counseling skills to help engaged couples who were about to be married. If a couple came to us and asked us to preside at their wedding, we were to require of the couple two or three pre-marital counseling sessions. In these pre-marital counseling sessions we would perform a emotional "check-up" on the health of the couple's relationship. Is the couple communicating openly? Are there any abusive or addictive behaviors that need to be dealt with? If one or both people have been previously divorced, have they come to terms with their feelings about the previous relationship? The pre-marital counseling sessions were meant to be beneficial to both the pastor and the couple. The pastor wanted to feel reasonably sure that the couple was in fact prepared for the rigors of a lifelong commitment to each other. The pre-marital interviews also helped the couple by pointing out where their relationship was strong and where there were areas in need of improvement. The intention behind the pre-marital counseling sessions was good, the goal being to better prepare a couple for marriage in the hope of decreasing any chance for divorce. But when I interviewed my first few couples, I ran into a problem.

READY FOR MARRIAGE?

How was I, the pastor, to know when a couple was ready for marriage or not? What was the measuring stick I should use to judge whether or not a couple's relationship was sound? The only thing I had to go on was the myth of the individual as it had been taught to me in my seminary counseling classes. The myth of the individual, as mentioned above, asserts that we must first actualize ourselves, satisfy our unmet ego needs, and learn to love ourselves before we can love others in a lasting way. The problem developed when I realized that *none* of the couples I interviewed were fully actualized individuals as described by the myth of the individual according to the popular model. Most of the couples were young and were several years away from developing the full emotional maturity demanded by the myth of the individual. Yet somehow I intuitively felt that most of the couples were ready to be married. If I followed the myth of the individual I had been taught, I would have had to say to most of the couples I interviewed that they should wait awhile before getting married. But such heavy handed advise would have been worthless. If a couple really wanted to get married, they would have no trouble finding another minister who would be willing to perform the wedding ceremony. So what was I to do? I decided to trash the popular model I had been taught, and instead trust my intuition that most of the couples I interviewed were indeed ready for marriage.

TWO SUGGESTIONS FOR MARRIAGE

As a result of interviews I have done with engaged couples, I have found two distinct characteristics in their relationships that help me conclude they are ready for marriage. The first characteristic is that both people are capable of intimacy. As I commented in the chapter on friendship, intimacy is the ability to share your fears, pains, hopes, and joys with others and to receive the same from others. This is where the myth of the individual is most helpful. The main point of the myth of the individual is that there needs to be a minimal level of emotional health before we can successfully engage in long term love relationships. If we carry heavy burdens from our past, such as emotional, physical, sexual and/or substance abuse, these burdens can impede our ability to be intimate with others. Where I part ways with the myth of the individual is just where in the journey towards emotional health we can learn to be intimate with others. I do not think we have to wait until we are fully actualized or have completely worked through our dysfunctions to attain intimacy. The skills that produce intimacy can be learned relatively easily by almost anyone. If we do not know how to be intimate with other people, there are a number of ways we can learn. We could choose a friend that we trust and begin a conscious effort to share concerns on a regular basis. We could also find a new "family of affiliation" as Bradshaw calls them.[66] Our new family of affiliation could be a therapy group, prayer group, or a support group that meets to help people with a common need. The hardest part about intimacy is finding the courage to risk intimacy in the first place. Fortunately, as we risk being intimate with others, in time it will come more easily.

The second characteristic I look for in an engaged couple is the openness of both people to the reality that they will each grow and change through the years. When I interview engaged couples, I make it clear to them that the person they are marrying will not be the same person they are married to five or ten years from now. Whether we like it or not, we will change not only physically but also emotionally and spiritually as the years go by. Married couples can either fight the process of change or cooperate with the process of change, but they cannot prevent it. If a couple chooses to fight the process of change, chances are that the marriage will not survive. What I specifically look for in couples I interview is the realization that they *will* change with time, and the belief in each other that will sustain them through those changes. "I believe in you. I believe in who you are and in who you can become." Once again this was a place where I had to part ways with the myth of the individual.

The myth of the individual holds that we *first* actualize ourselves and then we are capable of sustaining a lasting love relationship. I maintain that it is *within* our lasting love relationships, such as marriage, that we learn to mature emotionally and spiritually. Spiritual and emotional growth are not limited to the domain of spiritual love. I do not believe that romantic or marital love can be maintained without the knowledge of and commitment to the spiritual and emotional growth of our partner and ourself. Most often it is in love relationships that the issues of spiritual and emotional growth come up. And it is usually in love relationships that we can successfully work through our emotional growth. What the myth of the individual is lacking is the community of two or more that is necessary for achieving emotional and spiritual maturity. What the myth of the individual lacks is spiritual love.

In summary, I found two characteristics necessary for an engaged couple to win my confidence in the viability of their marriage. First, both partners must have the ability to be intimate with each other. Second, both partners need to be aware of and committed to sustaining the inevitable emotional and spiritual changes they will go through together. The myth of the individual points to the necessity of the first item, the ability of both partners to be intimate. What the myth of the individual lacks is the realization of the need for a community of two to facilitate our growth to emotional and spiritual maturity. Having answered the question of what is necessary to sustain a marriage, I must now turn to the unpleasant but companion question: When is a marriage no longer viable? In other words, when does divorce seem to be the only option left to a married couple?

WHEN MARRIAGE NO LONGER WORKS

To answer the complex question of when is a marriage no longer viable, I must preclude some extreme circumstances. I am assuming that there is not a problem of spouse or child abuse, financial neglect, and/or substance abuse. Any or all of these extreme situations would be grounds for termination of a marriage if there is no hope of working out these problems. By "no hope" I mean that the partners are unwilling or unable to come to terms with the dynamics of their relationship that fuel and sustain such destructive behaviors. Assuming then that there are no extreme and mitigating circumstances present, what causes a marriage to be no longer viable? A marriage becomes unviable when one or both partners are no longer willing to commit themselves to each others' spiritual and emotional growth.[67]

What do I mean by marriage partners being committed to each others' emotional and spiritual growth? There are three important aspects of emotional and spiritual growth in a marriage: Two partners in a marriage are usually at different levels of spiritual development, each grow at different rates, and each has their own mode of learning how to grow.

DIFFERENCES IN SPIRITUAL GROWTH

Very seldom will you find two people at the same level of spiritual development. Even if both partners are the same age and of the same religious and social background, there will be differences in their respective levels of spiritual development. This is neither good nor bad, simply a fact of life. As to what constitutes the various stages of spiritual development, the actual number depends on the writer consulted. John of the Cross talks of four stages,[68] Teresa of Avila describes seven stages.[69] I make a distinction between spiritual and emotional growth. While the two are definitely related, they are not the same. The method of attaining spiritual growth that I advocate involves the regular practice of a particular form of prayer. While therapy will touch on many of the issues involved with one's spiritual development, therapy by itself is not enough to constitute spiritual growth.[70]

The level of a person's spiritual development can range from occasional petitionary prayers offered by rote to regular practice of contemplative prayer. A difference in the levels of spiritual development does not in and of itself constitute an unviable marriage. A couple can still maintain intimacy without being at the same level of spiritual development. Part of the commitment of love is to provide sanctuary that gives a person the necessary safety he or she needs to risk and practice new forms of behavior, attitudes, and values that will enhance spiritual growth. Sanctuary can only be found when two people have come to believe in each other as they are and believe in what they can become. Without this mutual, almost paradoxical acceptance of each other, sanctuary cannot be found nor can spiritual growth be maintained.

Another difference that will occur is that people grow spiritually at different rates. Some who begin a regular practice of prayer may speed ahead in a few weeks time to experience the deep quiet of centering prayer. Still others may take months before they reach the deeper levels of meditation. Once again, there is nothing wrong with this variation in rates of spiritual growth. The variations are simply a fact of life in our day to day existence. It helps to keep in mind that we are not in control of our spiritual growth. The Holy Spirit sets the pace and timing for each of us.

A third important aspect of spiritual growth is that people will learn to grow in different modes. By mode I mean a person's primary way of processing information. One person may learn from reading books. Another may learn best by attending a public seminar. Yet another person may learn from one-on-one attention by a Spiritual Director. The important point is to be aware of your own particular mode of learning and the mode of your partner.[71] If varieties in modes are not mutually accepted, spiritual growth will be very difficult indeed.

I cannot emphasize enough how important it is to recognize variations in the ways of spiritual growth. It has been my sad experience, both personally and professionally, to see many love relationships unnecessarily ended for lack of appreciation regarding the differences in a couple's level, rate, and mode of spiritual growth. Quite often there are other complicating problems within a marriage in addition to the lack of awareness about spiritual growth. But without an understanding of the need for spiritual growth within marital love, other problems within a marriage are much more difficult to resolve.

How do you handle the frustration that inevitably comes with differences in a couple's spiritual growth? By maintaining friends outside the marriage, of both the same and opposite sex. In the chapter on friendship I mentioned Hugh Prather's idea that the one special companion for life we seem unable to find is really a conglomerate of the best traits from several friends we have known in the past. We each need breathing space in our marriages by spending time with people who are of the same level, rate, and mode of spiritual growth as we are. This illustrates the critical need for maintaining friendships outside of marriage. This is also a crucial reason for *not* expecting your spouse to be your best friend. As one comedian put it, "My wife keeps telling me I am her best friend. But all she does is complain about her husband." How can you expect your spouse to withstand your frustrations about their normal and different state of spiritual growth as compared to your own? To expect this is naive at best, cruel at worst.

Granted that a couple understands their differences in spiritual growth, we must return to our original question. When does a marriage become no longer viable? When one or both partners are no longer willing to provide the sense of sanctuary, practice the intimacy, and maintain belief in each other that are necessary to enhance spiritual growth.[72] I emphasize the word 'willing' because there are circumstances when maintaining commitment to spiritual growth may be difficult. Examples that come to mind are severe illness striking one of the partners, or that one's spouse may travel a great deal. Assuming, however, that all other things are equal, when a couple loses the willingness to maintain the conditions for spiritual growth, the loss of the marriage may not be far behind. Why is this? Because, as I have defined it, the primary reason that people marry is to sustain needs that can only be met by one special person. The lifetime commitment is necessary to build the trust and stability needed for the material conditions of love, as well as to provide the possibility of having children. Without an awareness of the need for and commitment to spiritual growth in a marriage, the ability for two partners to sustain each other in a long term commitment becomes problematic. All of the conditions I have listed in chapter one about being in love are needed not only for spiritual growth but for other aspects of the marital relationship as well. If the conditions for spiritual growth are not satisfied, then chances are that other areas of a marriage are being neglected as well.

In an ideal world we would realize the need for spiritual growth as we enter into marriage. Unfortunately, most of us learn these lessons the hard way as we stumble along, working and growing with our partners a day at a time. An important question will occur sometime in the life of most marriages. Where does family love fit into marital love?

MARRIAGE & FAMILY LOVE

The question of family love comes up most often regarding children. Before we were anything else, most of us came into the world as members of a particular family. And our experiences of family love, for better or for worse, greatly shaped our expectations about the other loves, particularly marital love. Our behavior in marital love will be greatly influenced by the behavior of our parents. So the question of family love engages marital love from two directions. Our prior experience of family love will greatly influence our experience of marital love. And our experience of family love will greatly affect the way we love our children. So what is family love? Before I give my definition I should issue a note of caution to the reader. I have only experienced one half of family love, when I was a child in my parents' household. I have never had children of my own, though some day I hope to do so. Since I have not experienced family love as a parent would, I can only speculate how family love is applied as a parent. I am sure that those readers who are parents could give me much practical advice on parenting and family love. With that warning in mind, here is my definition of family love.

FAMILY LOVE DEFINED

FAMILY LOVE: a love which, at first, is based on biological need, eventually is characterized by a combination of friendship and spiritual love.

As I have done before, let us look at this definition phrase by phrase.

At First, Based on Biological Need. It seems self-evident that newborn humans are completely dependent upon their parents for survival. Certainly there is a love that is a part of the infant/parent bond, although the bond is primarily determined by the biological needs of the infant. So family love does have its origin in a "need" relationship. It is not always this way, however, for the infant does grow up. Within a few years, the child learns to speak and think for itself. The biological-need basis of the child-parent bond will still be present even into the teenage years of a child's growth. Eventually, though, the biological-need basis of family love gradually recedes into the background. Somewhere along the way, family love takes on a different character.

Characterized by a Combination of Friendship and Spiritual Love. As a child learns to think and feel more on its own, the parent-child relationship begins to change. Parents and child begin to communicate with each other, sharing their own experiences. I would describe this relationship, in part at least, as a friendship between parent and child. The biological-need basis of family love will limit the "equal regard" aspect of friendship in a child's earliest years. But "equal regard" can be an ideal towards which the parent-child relationship can evolve as the child reaches young adulthood. "Respectful distance" will be developed with a vengeance by the child when adolescence rolls around. But since each child will have a unique personality to express, "respectful distance" is also a practical expedient for parents as well. Parents cannot expect their children to be exact replicas of themselves in all, or even most things. For example, while one parent may excel in sports, they may find their offspring does not have the slightest interest in sports. "Kindness and solicitude" would be a part of the parent-child relationship at any age.

Spiritual love is a part of family love from the very beginning. Spiritual love involves not only instruction in the way of formal religion. More importantly, spiritual love involves showing a child how they can draw near to and experience the presence of God through prayer. Contemplation as a prayer form may not be appropriate until the child is at least in their early teens. It is possible they can be taught other forms of prayer such as petitionary prayer, and prayers of praise and adoration. Ideally, a child would learn of the need for spiritual growth in love from their experience of family love. The parents would set an example by encouraging each other's spiritual growth. Hopefully the children would come to expect the same in their own love relationships.

It may be objected that my description of family love as being a combination of friendship and spiritual love is too idealistic, that it is unattainable in practice. I would argue that my definition of family love is and is not idealistic. It is idealistic because so many people have not experienced family love in the way I have described it. Yet, my definition of family love is not idealistic because I have experienced it that way myself. Within my own immediate family and across generations, my experience of family love has been primarily a combination of friendship and spiritual love. So I know from my own experience, at least, that family love is attainable as I have defined it. But why do so many people fail to experience family love as friendship and spiritual love? I honestly do not know. Is it possible that more people can experience family love as friendship and spiritual love? I certainly believe so, for that is a major reason for my writing this book. Perhaps it would help if I clarify what the expectations would be for someone who has been raised with family love as I have defined it.

Let us return to the myth of the individual. At least implicitly, the expectation is that our goal in family love should be to raise children who have *no* dysfunction and who become completely self-actualized by the time they reach young adulthood. I believe this goal is impossible to achieve. Part of the problem is the slippery term 'dysfunction." If by "no dysfunction" we mean the absence of physical, sexual, emotional, and/or substance abuse, then I heartily agree. We can and should seek to raise children free of dysfunction. However, if "no dysfunction" means the absence of fears and insecurities, then I believe that is an impossible goal. There is not a person on the face of the earth who does not struggle with fears and insecurities to some degree. I grew up with family love as a combination of friendship and spiritual love, and I have my own insecurities with which I must contend. Because my parents are imperfect humans, I inherited some of their fears and insecurities in addition to their giving me a very positive experience of family love. If percentages can be assigned to such things, I would guess my parents gave me an 80%-20% split, 80% functional, 20% leftover fears and insecurities for me to work through. Unlike some therapeutic strategies, though, I do not focus on the 20% of unresolved personal issues and angrily blame my parents for being lousy providers.[73] Instead, I look upon my 80% functional level as my parents' legacy of love to me. The 80% functional level they bequeathed to me enables me to work through the 20% of leftover personal issues. I was able to take responsibility for my own emotional and spiritual health and start to follow my own path to maturity thanks to the 80% functional level of health that my parents gave to me.

This 80%-20% split seems a more realistic goal to strive for than vain efforts to achieve the fully actualized self of the myth of the individual.[74] Perhaps the myth of the individual can once again be amended, but this time by community love instead of by spiritual love. Forgiveness and reconciliation are learned and practiced within community, whether it is a family or religious community. If we can reconcile ourselves to the fact we cannot attain the mythical perfection of self-actualization; if we can forgive ourselves for being imperfect parents and the children of imperfect parents,[75] then an 80%-20% split in function/dysfunction is a realistic goal that is well within the reach of many people. Family love, friendship, marital and romantic love augmented by spiritual love and community love become viable goals instead of envied ideals beyond our reach.

CHAPTER EIGHT

HAPPINESS

"Agape liberates the other loves so they may be experienced in a more fulfilling way."

Jill has been feeling restless about her life in recent weeks, but she does not know why. She is successful in her job as an accountant, and has been dating Ron for three years. They are talking about getting engaged and both are very excited about it. Jill also has several friends she sees regularly outside of work, so nothing seemed to be missing in her life. Yet when she is alone and taking inventory of her life, she feels a vague sadness about it all. She instinctively wants to go somewhere but she does not know where. She wants to do something but she does not know what.

Jill first noticed this vague sadness and restlessness when Donna, her best friend Mary's mother, passed away. Donna had been an active woman all of her life. She had successfully run her own company for years. In her retirement she was always spending time with friends or working on her favorite charity projects. All of this came to an end when Donna suffered a severe stroke at the age of 68. She never recovered and wasted away for a year in a nursing home before she finally died. Like a good friend, Jill was there for Mary through the whole ordeal. It wasn't until after Donna's funeral that Jill realized how much it had affected her.

It scared Jill to see an active person like Donna struck down so suddenly. Jill is also disturbed at how sad and lethargic Mary is now, a year after her mother's death. What scares Jill is that she sees herself in both Mary and her mother Donna.

Jill has never given much thought to old age. But her own parents are getting older now and will someday pass on. She panics at the thought of her parents lives ending like Donna's. It seems like such a waste that someone's life should end the way Donna's did. All of those productive years and what does it add up to? A body that fails you and a slow lingering death.

Jill has never been very religious but she finds herself wondering about things she has not thought of since childhood. Is there really a God? Does God care about us? Is there life beyond death? Or is this fragile life all we have? A few years of activity, ending in physical incapacitation and death? Jill believes she should feel happy with her life but instead she feels that vague sadness. Most important of all, she has Ron who wants to spend his life with her. This more than anything should make her happy. But even her love for Ron is not enough to overcome the sadness she feels. If love does not make her happy then what in the world will?

The questions facing Jill about love, happiness and death are not abstract questions found only in philosophy classes. They are very basic, practical concerns about how to live one's life. The answers Jill finds, if any, can make the difference between enduring life as if it were a long race we have no choice in running, or living with a sense of freedom and joy. Where do we begin to answer Jill's questions about love, death and happiness?

Edna St. Vincent Millay wrote a line in a sonnet that could have been personally directed to Jill :"Love is not all."[76] A love relationship, while important for our happiness, is not enough to make for happiness. So what is happiness if it is neither love nor found in love?

HAPPINESS DEFINED

I realize I am treading on tenuous ground in attempting to define happiness. Greater spirits than I have tried to define happiness and met with mixed results at best. But a workable understanding of happiness will help us keep the different loves in proper perspective. If we expect our love relationships to give us something they cannot provide, we can only come to grief. So without further ado, here is my definition of happiness.

HAPPINESS: The belief that one is part of a Process or Plan that extends beyond one's own needs and aspirations, that will have a positive impact on other peoples' lives, and will continue after one's death.

As before, let us look at this definition carefully.

That extends beyond one's own needs and aspirations. It seems to be commonplace wisdom anymore that getting everything we want in life, particularly of a material nature, does not make for happiness. Witness the usually disparaging acronym 'yuppy' and how the material acquisitiveness of the eighties mellowed to a search for spiritual meaning in the nineties.[77] But there is more involved in this phrase from my definition than just realizing the limits of material gain.

One version of happiness is found in the saying "moderation in all things." The belief is that if we learn to live a controlled or moderated existence within our own limits, we will find happiness.[78] The limits described include our social and political circumstances, as well as self-imposed limits to our desires and ambitions. If we concentrate on our small corner of the world, such as home and family, we will find happiness. There are problems with the view of happiness as moderation in all things, however.

HAPPINESS IS MORE THAN MODERATION IN ALL THINGS

One major problem with the idea of happiness as moderation is that it breeds a narrow, even fragmented view of the world. If we concentrate upon our own needs, we have little or no incentive to improve the lot of other people less fortunate than us. Happiness as moderation becomes a commodity that we need not spread around to others beyond our immediate circle of friends and family. Happiness as moderation easily slides into narcissism clothed in moral attire.

Jill's situation is a good example of the limitations of happiness as moderation. Her life is neatly divided into separate compartments: boyfriend, job, friends. Her life seems to be complete but she doe not feel it is complete. The neat little compartments that constitute Jill's life have been shattered by the messy realities of Donna's illness and death. Watching Mary and her mother's slow death shook Jill's illusion of a complete life. Jill's sense of sadness and feeling that she wants to go somewhere and do something is her subconscious rebelling against her fragmented life.

Another major drawback to the idea of happiness as moderation is that in times of social and political upheaval, happiness as moderation is beyond the reach of many or even most people.[79] I tend to look upon our present era, both domestically and internationally, as one that qualifies as "political and social upheaval." In these uncertain times, happiness must involve more than moderation within our own individual lives. Jill is fortunate that she is relatively well off financially, but even in her material circumstances she is not happy. How much more difficult would it be for her if she lost her job? And what of the many people who have and will lose their jobs to changing world markets, or the ever increasing number of wars being fought around the world? Surely happiness must consist of more than a stable means of livelihood.

A PLAN OR PROCESS?

The belief that one is part of a Process or Plan. The only way I know of to overcome the inherent narrowness of the happiness as moderation view is to broaden our vision of life. A great many people feel the need to belong to something greater than themselves. It could be religion, as this part of the definition obviously describes. Or it might be a social or political movement, an organization, even the latest cultural fashions. Anything that gives us some feeling of being a part of something greater than ourselves is a possible candidate. Jill is beginning to face up to her need to belong to something greater than her own individual existence. The questions she is asking about God, life after death, and is there something more to life, will all lead her to the need to belong to something greater than herself. She needs some reassurance about the purpose of life in general as she faces up to her own mortality in particular.

I have opted for a religious solution to the questions Jill is asking. I use the ambiguous terms "Process or Plan" because I think happiness can be reached in a number of ways. The Eastern religions with which I am familiar, such as Buddhism and Taoism, describe the ultimate scheme of things as a Process. Tao is always moving and changing,[80] and the five skandhas of Buddhism are shifting and mixing in new combinations.[81] The term "Plan" would encompass the various notions of Divine Providence found in the Western religions of Judaism, Christianity, and Islam. While I have my own preferences, I do not feel I can adjudicate which tradition makes for the greatest happiness. So I include both "Process" and "Plan" in my definition of happiness.

Some personal experience also leads me to include both "Process" and "Plan" in my definition of happiness. My own experience of prayer and guidance in prayer has been both frustrating and exhilarating. It has been frustrating because sometimes I think there is a Plan, other times merely an open ended Process. I keep moving between Plan and Process in my own theological outlook regarding God and his place in the world. Yet my experience of prayer and guidance has also been exhilarating. The many times I have "accidentally" met interesting people, or "just happened" to run across a book or article I needed for writing this book are too numerous to be coincidence. I have felt the presence of a guiding purpose in my life too many times to completely dismiss the idea that God has a Plan of some sort. Thus I include "Process" and "Plan" to cover my own varied experiences of God and prayer.

Jill has a wide range of religion options from which to choose. Her lack of religious background will make it difficult for her to know where to start. But at least she sees that her questions about love, happiness and death all come from natural events in her life. The question of what makes for happiness if not love comes from her relationship with Ron. The questions about God and life after death come out of her experience of Donna's illness and death. Jill displays the "it won't happen to me" attitude so many of us have from our younger years. This is especially true if people come from backgrounds where there has been little long term illness or financial hardship. The idyllic safety of childhood becomes an expectation, even a demand that life continues to be safe and predictable in adulthood. But sooner or later the messiness and unpredictability of life breaks through as it has for Jill. Watching Donna's lingering death and its affect on Mary changed Jill's vision of life forever. Whether Jill chooses a religion that offers a Plan or Process, the vision of life she eventually chooses will hopefully give her positive answers to the questions she is asking.

That will have a positive impact on other peoples' lives. If happiness is being part of a Process or Plan that extends beyond ourselves, hopefully such a Process or Plan will have a positive impact on the lives of others. Within our own circle of friends and family, we can have a visible impact. But many people feel a desire to "do something more" with their lives. They want to make a difference by leaving the world in better shape than how they found it to be. What "do something more" means specifically will vary from person to person. It could range from volunteer service for a charity organization to a complete change in career.

A NEED TO DO SOMETHING MORE

Jill is beginning to feel the need to "do something more" in two ways. First, she has always admired Donna for the active life she led such as running her own business and her charity work. Donna's death may be the catalyst that leads Jill to become more active in her own life. Second, a decision by Jill to become more active will help alleviate the restlessness she has been feeling. Instead of not knowing where to go and what to do in response to her restlessness, Jill can take charge of her life and give it a sense of direction and purpose. The need to "do something more" felt by Jill and others is really the flip side of our need for community.

In the chapter on community love I discussed our need for a community that encourages spiritual growth. Our need for community goes beyond meeting our own growth needs, however. We belong to a community not only to meet our needs, we also belong to a community in order to give. Jill is feeling the need to give to others, to see that her life has meaning beyond her own immediate life and friends. She may not be at a point where she can clearly articulate that need, but she is well on her way to doing so. Belonging to a community, giving to a community helps us feel connected to something greater than ourselves. To know that what we do will have an effect beyond our immediate circle of acquaintances adds to our sense of happiness.

LIFE AFTER DEATH?

And will continue after one's death. How does happiness stand up to the ultimate question, death? Our happiness will be on shaky ground if the effect we have upon the world perishes when we do. If our impact and our happiness are limited to the span of our own lifetime, there is little incentive or hope for seeking happiness in the first place. This brings us to a very crucial characteristic of happiness: We cannot find lasting and complete happiness within our earthly existence. We can find some happiness, feel it, experience it in this life, but it will never be quite enough. One author describes this aspect of happiness as "transcending anticipation."[82] While we will find happiness in this life, we will always be less than satisfied and feel that there must be something more. Jill is beginning to see, however vaguely, that she might not find a complete sense of happiness in this world. The questioning occasioned by Donna's death has forced Jill to start thinking about religious questions for the first time in her adult life. Is there a God? Is there life after death? She has also begun to realize that no matter how much she loves Ron, this will not completely satisfy her desire for "something more" in the way of meaning or happiness.

The "something more" that Jill is seeking comes from being part of a Process or Plan. By participating in a Process or Plan that extends beyond our life and death, we can find satisfaction that the efforts we make in this life will continue beyond our own death. This is the only way our transcendent anticipation will ever be fulfilled. Jill senses that she cannot be happy if a painful and lingering death is all that awaits her at the end of her life. Such an end is an insult to the kind of life Donna lived and the kind of person she had been. How could Jill ever be satisfied with that? How could anyone for that matter? Such concerns naturally lead to religious questions about existence and hopefully some religious answers.

All of this leads to the inevitable question of whether or not *we* continue in some way after death. I believe that we do continue after death, and I will have more to say on that in the next chapter. In relation to happiness, I believe that some kind of afterlife is needed to fulfill the transcending anticipation of happiness. When we feel unfulfilled by earthly experiences of happiness, these glimpses of incomplete happiness are signs of a greater happiness yet to come. The happiness we now experience in part will be more fully known beyond this life. Whether a life beyond death is characterized by Nirvana or Heaven, I must leave as an open question. But our hope of finding happiness in this life rests upon the awareness and experience of a Process or Plan that extends beyond our earthly existence.

LOVE AND HAPPINESS

How does this definition of happiness relate to the different loves? Happiness, as I have defined it, should remove the tremendous pressure of expectations we place upon our love relationships. So many people look to their love relationships, especially marriage, to give them the happiness they cannot find on their own. Jill is on the verge of seeing this truth as she realizes her relationship with Ron will not fill the emptiness she feels in her life. This realization on Jill's part may very well be the saving grace of her future marriage to Ron. It is sad that so many people do not share Jill's insight, for if love is not enough to provide happiness, then there must be many frustrated lovers in the world. The belief that love brings happiness is left over from the ideology of romantic love that tells us we will live happily ever after if we can only find the right person with whom to spend our life. If we realize that love by itself will *not* bring happiness, then hopefully we will be more tolerant of the imperfections of those we love. If our relationships have their problems, if those we love do not always meet our expectations, we have not lost our only chance for happiness. When we do not expect love to give us the happiness we seek there will be more room for forgiveness of the imperfections and problems that always accompany love. Having more forgiveness and tolerance in our love relationships by *not* expecting them to make us happy may have the paradoxical effect of producing *more* happiness: the realization that love is not enough for happiness may very well save many relationships from needlessly breaking up. While love will be a part of our happiness, happiness encompasses far more than just our love relationships.

CHAPTER NINE

ON LOVE, DEATH, AND HOPE

"The Creator gives us a point of light to focus upon-our love endures beyond death, our loved ones endure beyond death."

In the previous chapters I have tried to give definition to the different loves we experience in life. In this last and final chapter I will try to deal with perhaps the most difficult question about love: What happens to love when death comes calling?

To answer this question, it helps to bring to mind the one experience of death that is almost universal to us the living, and that is the funeral. I have been on both sides of the funeral ceremony, as presiding pastor and as mourner. A funeral stirs up emotions like no other experience of which I can think. We come face to face with our own mortality and it is never a pleasant experience. People hold funerals for all kinds of reasons. Some do so for religious reasons, others because they feel the departed would want it, still others do it simply out of habit. But in my experience, there is one reason more than others why people hold funerals for those they have lost: They cannot forget the ones they loved and lost to death.

Is it realistic or prudent to remember, to memorialize, to reminisce about those we loved and lost to death? If it is true that "when you're dead, you're dead," funerals should be a final act of letting go of the ones we love. We remember the departed, we share a few kind thoughts about their time on earth, and then we get on with our lives. We should let go of our loved one and our love for them. Once they are gone from our lives there seems little point in dwelling upon them. To keep remembering, to keep loving even after death has claimed them is only torture for the living over someone, something we can never get back. So the prudent thing to do about love in the face of death is to let go and get on with our lives... Or is it?

If the above description is the primary purpose and goal of funerals, I have yet to see it succeed. Most of the people I know who have lost loved ones to death have continued to love and remember their departed. Even after we have gone through the necessary and healing stages of grief, our love remains alive. This continuance of love even in the face of death may be simply a case of mass denial, a matter of wishful thinking by most of humanity. The continuance of love in the face of death could be an attempt to avoid the awful truth that "when you're dead, you're dead." But then that is the dilemma of love in the face of death. There is the realist position of "when you're dead, you're dead." And then there is the reality of love continuing in the face of death.

It is my own belief that the continuance of love by the living for those claimed by death is not a matter of wishful thinking. On the contrary, I believe it is a positive clue, a telling us of things we can only dimly comprehend in this life. I can prove neither the existence of God nor the reality of life after death. But the widespread continuance of love in the face of death comes close in my way of thinking. I believe our stubbornness, even inability to stop loving those who have died is a way that God speaks to us. Our continued love for those we have lost to death is a signpost, a gentle nudge to reassure us that there *is* more beyond death. On this side of the valley of the shadow of death, our love continues beyond the death of our family, romantic partners, and friends. This is an inkling of a reality greater than ourselves; our love endures beyond death, our loved ones endure beyond death.

I believe it is the deepest insight of the Christian faith that love is the greatest bond we can share with each other in this life. And by extension, love is the greatest bond we can share with God in this life and beyond death. So in the midst of our love that refuses to yield in the face of death, I find a basis for hope. The endurance of love in the face of death is a hopeful sign that the Creator of love leaves for us. It is a point of light for us to focus upon--our love endures beyond death, our loved ones endure beyond death. For now we can only see these things dimly in the mirror of our earthly loves. Someday we will fully know and understand this Love face to face.

About the Author

Craig Owen is Assistant Professor of Religion & Philosophy and College Chaplain at a small college in the Southeast. When he is not teaching or writing, he enjoys photography, performing his original music and hiking with his wife, Karen.

Endnotes

1. Eugene C. Kennedy, <u>Believing</u> (Garden City, NY: Doubleday, 1974), 77.

2. Erich Fromm, <u>The Art of Loving</u> (New York: Harper & Row, 1974), 34.

3. Anne Tyler, <u>The Accidental Tourist</u> (New York: Berkley Books, 1986), 307.

4. This is an expansion of Theodore Isaac Rubin's definition of love. See <u>Reconciliations</u> (New York: Viking Press, 1980), 241.

5. Diogenes Allen, <u>Love: Christian Romance, Marriage, Friendship</u> (Cambridge, MA: Cowley Publications, 1987), 38.

6. Ibid.

7. Ibid., 97.

8. Jerry Greenwald, <u>Creative Intimacy</u> (New York: Jove Books, 1978), 34.

9. Hugh Prather, <u>Notes on Love and Courage</u> (Garden City, NY: Doubleday, 1977).

10. Allen, <u>Love</u>, 4. The ideology of romantic love would have us believe that our primary purpose in life is to find that one special love, marry them, and live happily ever after.

11. See Greenwald, <u>Creative Intimacy</u>; David Kiersey & Marilyn Bates, <u>Please Understand Me</u> (Delmar, CA: Prometheus Nemesis, 1978); and George R. Bach & Peter Wyden, <u>The Intimate Enemy: How to Fight Fair in Love and Marriage</u> (New York: Avon Books, 1970).

12. Wing-Tsit Chan translates it as "cunning" or "desire." I paraphrase it as "scheming ambition." See <u>The Way of Lao Tzu</u> (Indianapolis: Bobbs-Merrill Co., Inc., 1962), 103.

13. Kenneth William Morgan, ed., <u>The Path of the Buddha</u> (New York: Ronald Press Co., 1956), 111.

14. Eph. 4:22

15. Morgan, <u>Path of the Buddha</u>, 111.

16. Robert C. Solomon, <u>About Love: Reinventing Romance For Our Times</u> (New York: Simon & Schuster, Inc., 1988), 62-64.

17. Ibid., 235.

18. Ibid., 24.

19. Ibid., Ch. 3. My discussion on falling in love, being in love, and infatuation is condensed from Solomon's extended discussion.

20. Ibid., 83-88.

21. Dean C. Delis and Cassandra Phillips, <u>The Passion Paradox</u> (New York: Bantam Books, 1990), 35-36, 90-91.

22.Ibid.

23.Ibid.

24.Ibid., 165.

25.Ibid., 191.

26.Solomon, About Love, 166.

27.Ibid., 342-343.

28.This definition of **agape** is an expansion of M. Scott Peck's definition of love. See The Road Less Traveled, (New York: Simon & Schuster, 1979), 81.

29.Allen, Love, 25-26.

30. Robert Wuthnow, "The Church: Can It Sustain Community?," The World and I, Vol. 5, No. 10, 1990: 514.

31.Ibid., 514-515.

32.Ibid., 515-516.

33.Ibid., 516-517.

34.Ibid.

35.Gustaf Aulen, Christus Victor (New York: MacMillan Publishing Co., 1969), 79.

36.Thomas Keating, Open Mind, Open Heart (Amity, N.Y.: Amity House, 1986), 93.

37.Thomas Merton, New Seeds of Contemplation (New York: New Directions, 1972), 34-35.

38.Morton Hunt, The Compassionate Beast (New York: William Morrow & Co., Inc., 1990).

39.Ibid., 204.

40.Ibid., 203.

41.Ibid., 204.

42.Ibid.

43.Jerome Neu, "Jealous Thoughts," in Explaining Emotions, ed. Amelie Oskenberg Rorty (Berkeley: University of California Press, 1980), 451.

44.Ibid., 430.

45.Ibid., 433.

46.Ibid.

47.Ibid., 434.

48.Ibid.

[49] Ibid.

[50] Ibid., 431-432.

[51] Ibid., 454-455.

[52] Ibid., 456.

[53] Ibid.

[54] Ibid.

[55] Leila Tov-Ruach, "Jealousy, Attention, and Loss," in Rorty, Explaining Emotions, 471.

[56] Neu, "Jealous Thoughts," 432.

[57] Ibid., 432.

[58] Tov-Ruach, "Jealousy, Attention, and Loss," 470-471.

[59] Merton, New Seeds of Contemplation 35.

[60] Ibid., 57.

[61] Ibid., 76.

[62] Ibid., 60.

[63] C. S. Lewis, The Four Loves (New York: Harcourt, Brace, Jovanovich, Inc., 1960), 183-185.

[64] Charles L. Whitfield, Healing the Child Within (Deerfield Beach, FL: Health Communications, Inc., 1987), 2.

[65] Bellah, Habits of the Heart, 98.

[66] John Bradshaw, Bradshaw On: The Family (Deerfield Beach, FL: Health Communications, Inc., 1988), 200.

[67] I use the word 'willing' here with some reservation. What happens in the extreme circumstance where one of the partners becomes incapacitated from a catastrophic illness or accident? The incapacitated partner may not be willing or able to sustain the emotional or spiritual growth of their mate, but this hardly qualifies as grounds for terminating a marriage. I can only argue that here is a clear example of how emotional and spiritual growth, even in a marriage, depends on a community of two or more. The "or more" would come from friends, at the least, and ideally from a community founded on community love. Both the incapacitated partner and the ambient partner will have a greater than usual need for emotional and spiritual support from outside the marriage.

[68] St. John of the Cross, Ascent of Mount Carmel, 3rd rev. ed., (New York: Image Books, 1958).

[69] Teresa of Avila, The Interior Castle (New York: Paulist Press, 1979).

[70] "The focus in counseling is more on problem solving, of effecting better personal integration and adjustment in the process of human maturation. The focus in spiritual direction, on the other hand, is more on growth in prayer and charity [agape]." S. McCarty, "On Entering Spiritual Direction'" Review for Religious 35 (1976): 858. I see therapy focusing primarily upon correcting dysfunctional behavior and emotional growth. Spiritual direction and spiritual growth have as their goal the practice of prayer and agape. I think spiritual growth is the more comprehensive category, with emotional growth a subset of the larger goal of spiritual growth.

[71.]People display at least five distinct ways of thinking, gathering information, and solving problems: Synthetic, Idealistic, Pragmatic, Analytic and Realistic modes of thinking. See Allen F. Harrison and Robert M. Bramson, The Art of Thinking (New York: Berkley Books, 1984). A person's personality type will greatly affect the way he or she experiences and expresses their religious faith and spiritual growth. See W. Harold Grant, Magdala Thompson, and Thomas E. Clarke, From Image to Likeness (New York: Paulist Press, 1983).

[72.]Allen, Love, 110.

[73.]Melinda Blau, "Adult Children: Tied to the Past," American Health Vol. 9 No. 6 (July 1990): 58.

[74.]Ibid., 60.

[75.]Ibid., 65.

[76.]Edna St. Vincent Millay, Collected Sonnets (New York: Harper & Row, 1988), 99.

[77.]Kenneth L. Woodward, et. al., "A Time to Seek," Newsweek, 17 December 1990, 50.

[78.]Stephan Strasser, Phenomenology of Feeling: An Essay on the Phenomena of the Heart (Pittsburgh: Duquesne University Press, 1977), 349-350.

[79.]Ibid., 352.

[80.]Wing-Tsit Chan, Lao Tzu, 124, 160.

[81.]"According to Buddhist teaching, man consists of five 'heaps,' technically known as skandhas. They are : The Body, Feelings, Perceptions, Impulses and Emotions, and Acts of Consciousness...which make up the stuff of 'individuality.'" Edward Conze, Buddhism: Its Essence and Development (New York: Harper & Row, 1959), 14.

[82.]Strasser, Phenomenology of Feeling, 373.

Printed in the United States
47398LVS00005B/114

9 781585 004003